MORE TRAVELS IN A DONKEY TRAP

Anyone who read Daisy Baker's remarkable
story of how she acquired a donkey and trap
at the age of 76, and set forth to explore
the leafy lanes of Devon, will be delighted
to know that the intrepid traveller is still
travelling, and that Darkie is still tasting the
hedgerows.

In this sequel to the immensely popular
Travels in a Donkey Trap, Darkie and her
owner take a donkey holiday, an expedition
in search of a lost cat that is at the same time
a journey into the author's own memory as
she dreams and muses upon the mystery
that reconciles her present with her past.
Daisy Baker has an unerring eye for what is
beautiful and exciting in the simplest things,
and she manages to pack her few days'
journey through the deep summer lanes of the
West Country with suspense, joy, and
exhilaration. Yet what she most vividly
communicates to her readers is that rare and
extraordinary peace – the peace of her beloved
countryside, of her placid and kindly donkey,
and above all the inner peace of one who
has learned to enjoy her quiet and adventurous
late years.

**Also by the same author,
and available in Coronet Books:**

TRAVELS IN A DONKEY TRAP

More Travels in a Donkey Trap

Daisy Baker

ILLUSTRATED BY PAMELA MARA

CORONET BOOKS
Hodder and Stoughton.

First published 1976 by Souvenir Press Ltd
and simultaneously in Canada by Methuen

Coronet edition 1978

Printed and bound in Great Britain for
Hodder and Stoughton Paperbacks, a
division of Hodder and Stoughton Ltd.,
Mill Road, Dunton Green, Sevenoaks,
Kent (Editorial Office: 47 Bedford
Square, London, WC1 3DP) by
Hunt Barnard Printing Ltd., Aylesbury, Bucks.

ISBN 0 340 22305 7

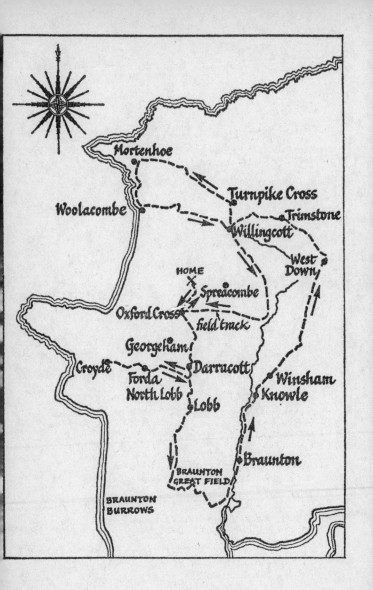

WE were imprisoned for weeks that summer, Darkie and I. Our jailers were the wind and rain. Darkie's exercise was stable to hedge; mine, even more limited, from bed to chair, fireside to window.

Freda laughed and said, 'Lovely weather! Better than going out when it's hot. If you wrap up you could go for miles.'

The wind, she said, was refreshing, and it was only necessary to get wet *outside* oneself. I agreed about the wind, but preferred to breathe the sweet freshness of it from the comparative shelter of the window. And Darkie, I knew, shared my dislike of being out in rain. Our slow journeys were not for such days as these. We were fair weather travellers.

And so I contented myself, thinking that in some ways we are alike, the donkey and I.

Then came a softer day when the wind was no more than the air breathing, and the rain had gone for a while. I walked out into the strange morning that was neither summer nor winter, spring nor autumn, but somehow contrived to be an odd mixture of each. Seldom had a day revealed to me such an identity of its own, such eccentricities. It had an allure for all its strangeness; an abundance of interest. In fact, there seemed even more to observe, to charm the eye and stimulate the imagination than on an ordinary day.

After the tempestuous weather, all around me seemed to be at rest, yet at the same time expectant. The sand-brown wheat field stood as motionless as the firm sand by the sea, as if it had never responded to the boisterous wind in wild tossing, nor made pools of light in the sun. But it was full of holes where the rain had beaten it – little indentations and great hollows. A sight to sadden when you thought of harvest time.

In the rowan tree stood a blackbird, poised in alert observation before taking a scarlet berry in his sharp yellow beak and swallowing it whole. The waist-high bracken stood down by the hedge, not a ripple of air to climb its green ladders of leaves. By the kitchen window were new sealed rosebuds that had somehow escaped being ripped off by the wind.

The donkey and the billy goat stood together in the centre of the field, not knowing whether soon they might bask in sunshine or again seek the shelter of the hedge. Around them the seeded grass on a patch none of the animals had grazed was so beaded with raindrops it was like a spread strawberry net of muslin. Wide, flat blades with pointed tips had become silvered spears.

Gone were the ballet dancer flowers of the columbines in the borders; shut up in the little brown houses on tall, straw-coloured stems were their tiny black seeds that jumped and rattled when brushed against as if eager to come rushing out to seek the earth and grow for another summer. The curved leaves of the columbines held raindrops as silver as a snail's trail.

We were all held in a strange atmosphere of remoteness, the garden and I, the field and the animals. It was like being on an island in a great isolation of sky. Nothing moved once I had paused, the blackbird had swallowed his berry, and the jumping seeds had settled as their stem ceased to sway.

The sky dominated the earth. Sky everywhere, as always here, but surely lower today, with its blanketing grey clouds without shape or form or distinction of any kind. A uniform greyness – yet, along the sky-line, light. Did they know too, all that stood with me, waiting?

And then suddenly it was there. Not wind again, or rain, and not yet sunshine, but an almost tangible something in the air, invisible yet felt, as if one might touch it.

A warmth was creeping into the atmosphere.

For this we had waited. With it the strangeness slowly melted away; a sense of relaxing came, of the earth stretching, of movement coming back into what had been a tableau.

King Billy sat down.

Now it was higher that light broke through; on the sky-line blackness. And like a strong swimmer in the sea of grey cloud above came the sun. A glimpse of blue at the same time sent me to the field fence.

'Enough blue to patch a sailor's pants, Darkie! Shall we go?'

She had not yet sat down, or moved. For her the day had still not established itself. Soon she would know.

'It's a day for donkeys,' I promised her. 'You'll see.'

I always talk to her. In fact, we talk to all the animals. Susy, with all the advantages of being a dog, interprets most words easily. The cats catch on to some when they benefit by doing so, and one, when spoken to about anything at all, will listen with rapt attention and pale green penetrating gaze, answering with tiny miaows.

'Nice goat day today,' Freda will say when she opens the goat house and the sun is coming up. One by one the goats step out to see for themselves. If it's 'not much of a goat day today' they wait for their bowls to be placed within doors.

The white rabbit answers to her name and comes in one straight run. She also knows exactly what 'Home' means.

However, it is Darkie, whose large receptive ears seem to be made for listening, to whom I mostly converse. I am flattered, perhaps, by the responsive movements of those ears, by the brightness in her dark eyes as she regards me, and the occasional nudge of her nose. She uses her ears for exclamations. 'Quite so!', 'Yes, let's!', and the various trivi-alities of conversation. Her eyes are herself, suggesting to me that her broad forehead stores much wisdom. When her nose enters into it as well she is either feeling playful or wishes to say, 'Come on, let's get on with it. Enough talk for one day.' I like to think she understands me as well as I understand her – or should it be the other way round?

Happily conscious that we were returning to summer on that morning born out of season, I went back to the house to prepare to go out. My spirits fell when Freda said, 'There's going to be more rain today according to the forecast.'

In my room I debated where to go, or even whether to go or not. There had been so few journeys that summer that I had no wish to be dissuaded now an apparent opportunity had come. It was not raining *now*, or blowing, and we would surely have time to go to the village and back before the rain came.

Yet Darkie was not keen. From my window I could see she was still standing motionless in the same spot. She would not go to browse down the field, or sit on her patch of earth.

Her ears looked disconsolate at their half-way angle. Was she too, like the forecasters, expecting rain?

I compromised by putting a mackintosh sheet in the cart for her and an umbrella for myself.

Now it was a morning of light and shade, with the ease of warmth and a ripple of summer air. Still encased in cloud a fleeting sun was pouring light on to the farther fields,

turning them into shimmering lakes against the shadowed grass in the nearer fields, and the bracken-covered banks, now so dark a green in late summer, looked almost black.

The warmth brought the butterflies, flitting in twos and threes around the garden. In less than a minute there were creamy white wings fluttering past, little bright browns and blues, and spread on the grey lichened trunk of the sycamore was a Red Admiral, colours more brilliant than I had ever seen, as if it had been that moment carved upon the tree and freshly painted. A newly emerged butterfly drying its wings – could the morning offer more?

Yet I paused more than once on my way across the garden, arms full of harness. A yellowhammer sat quite close on the field fence, head as bright as the hawkbit in the field. So slight was the ripple of air that the atmosphere retained its stillness, and I heard a woodpigeon's wings creak as he flew a field width away. A brown bird flying into the may tree down the field halted me. So sudden and sharp the thrill, so tantalisingly is one on tiptoe, for this was a stranger.

They often come, the strangers – single, unrecognised birds, possibly migrants, pausing briefly and passing on. But the brown bird so soon within the cover of the tree had in that glimpse reminded me of an owl. I had only seen white owls here, and then not often. I stood and stared down the field and saw movements within the tree, glimpses of brown, and then he flew – flew low as an owl would along by the hedge, but it was not an owl's flight. He was gone, a stranger passing, leaving me to ponder the mystery of his identity.

Then the garden was suddenly filled with the little melodies of many birds, all blending into one unbroken rhythm. To this accompaniment I went into the field, and then, returning to the house for something, walked under the trees and so disturbed them. A cloud of little finches rose from the twiggy, close-leaved sloe trees growing out of the stone wall, and circled above the feathery tips of the tall firs. For a moment I saw them individually, lingering over the garden on hesitant wings before taking off to the treeless fields. These were not our resident finches, but strangers passing by, as the brown bird had been.

And so, at last, to the task of harnessing. I wonder if car drivers ever dream of a chauffeur. Maybe they do as they cope with the frustrations of motoring on busy highways and the tensions involved. Darkie and I take quieter ways, only occasionally venturing further afield among the jam-packed cars of the summer visitors, so it is not the driving that troubles me. If I had a dream I sometimes think it would be not for a chauffeur, or donkey driver, but a groom.

To allot to someone else the stresses of straps and buckles, of easing a particular strap to the exact spot on that rotund belly where it will meet its buckle at the right hole for the security of the harness and the comfort of she who wears it!

'James! Bring the donkey cart!'

But there is no James, unless Eric or Freda take over, and if there were I can imagine sending him packing the first week. For to no James would I willingly relinquish this task, so personal to Darkie and establishing even closer contact between us. As with most tasks, the tedium of it is by no means all.

I was well aware, that summer day, with so doubtful a

sky, that by the time I had mounted the driving seat rain might be upon us. Like a child I anticipated all being well if we could only get *started*. To be prevented from going at all was unthinkable. I suppose Darkie sensed my mood, for her weather instinct was subdued by her instinct to respond, and she was at the field gate in no time, even forgoing her usual preliminary half circle round the field.

The tethered goats – tethered only temporarily to prevent them milling around the cart in a commotion of curiosity – watched the proceedings with their usual interest. Although they have seen the same thing happen many times, their interest never flags for a moment. The arrival of the cart in the field is the signal for them to converge. At first they want to inspect it, even to climb into it, but when the ropes restrain them they content themselves by standing quite still to watch.

After following Darkie's progress up the field with eager gaze, as if they would gladly give up an hour's grazing to change places with her, they do not miss a detail of the harnessing. I smile as I picture a trio of goats between the shafts, and wave to them when Darkie and I drive off. 'See you soon!'

Interest remains steady right until we are out of sight. I glance round to see they have turned to watch us, eyes bright with that particular goat sparkle of alertness, the white mother goat wearing what I always call her smiling expression.

At one time they, too, went for walks. They would follow willingly up the long lane between fields, eating as they went, careful to let no distance grow between themselves and the one they followed. But the lane is narrow and full grown billy goats become boisterous, so the practice had to be discontinued.

'See you soon, goats!' I called as Darkie and I drove off that day. There was still no sign of rain, and Darkie was now all set for the adventure of going out.

As we went down the lane I recaptured the old thrill of the reins in my hands as I sat up behind the donkey. For me the joy of being on the road again; for her a tranquil amble with satisfying hedge snacks. The grass, she believes, is sweeter beyond the field, and there is hazel in the hedges.

We went up the hill leading to the village, I enjoying the tranquillity of our pace and the opportunity for observation, Darkie with an eye for the best stopping places. Her pauses always occur at the exact spot where her questing nose can rummage out the choicest delicacies.

In much the same way do I search out the hedge as step by step we pass each inch of it. But I am looking for beauty, or seeking out any of the hedge population who may be visible. Darkie discovers oak leaves; I delight in a tiny oak apple, flushed red and quite unblemished. Darkie finds bramble leaves; I look down upon a spider's nest in the grass, leaning over the cart to be sure, with one finger gently touching the soft grey ball that might be only thistledown. It comes alive with a multitude of tumbling baby spiders, no larger than pinheads.

Perhaps it was a spider's nest I saw that day, or a small colony of ants which had grown those shining wings that look so large for their little bodies, or a bright caterpillar, or perhaps I only saw the grass move and heard a tantalising rustle from some inhabitant of the hedge who remained invisible. Looking as we went along, I was thinking of the pleasure of the journey itself.

I wondered what interesting little episode might come my way, for it is rare to go out with a donkey without something of interest occurring. I could have wished we were going further than the village, that I might indulge a dream and

13

set off on some longer journey, perhaps even putting up for a night or two.

'How about it, Darkie? Shall we play truant? Go adventuring?'

She cocked both ears at me, up and then down and then at their half-way angle. Puzzled? Probably. I gave her familiar words. 'Come on, then. Good girl.'

Tugging out a mouthful of grass, she took me to the top of the hill. Still it did not rain, and we made our steady way down the other side into the village street. Down the dip to the post office, and she waited by the churchyard wall, contentedly rubbing her neck on one of the shafts of the cart, while I collected my pension.

From here we drove around the turnings to look at cottage gardens – I to look, that is, she to stretch desirous nose towards neat hedges, which this time she was not permitted to sample. I let her stop at a convenient place where she crunched at her favourite wide-bladed grass on a verge.

It was a quiet hour, the shop just closing for lunch, and when the cows had ambled softly by, the black and white farm dog slipping past their hooves like a shadow, and the little old man with the rustic stick had brought up the rear, nodding at me with merry grin, the street was empty.

The clock on the old grey church chimed. I watched the swallows slip under thatched eaves to a hidden nest, and on a telephone wire saw twin young ones, all quivering with life and appetite, being fed by the parent bird, who did not alight, but poised in the air in front of them with dipping beak, rising again in zig-zag flight for another tongueful of insects.

The swallow's movements lulled me almost to drowsing until I noticed a girl coming down the street. She carried a basket of bottles and walked quickly. As she drew level with the cart I glanced down, expecting to exchange a smile and a greeting, which is customary in the village street, even when you do not know the other person. There was no answering glance, however, and she appeared not to notice the donkey. In that one glimpse of her face I saw the tense frown and knew that she did not see the swallows either, which struck me as quite sad. In this age of artificially induced emotions and mass-produced entertainment the 'real thing' is so often overlooked; part of the background, if that. I wondered if it

14

is always that 'we have no time to stand and stare'. Rather, I think, that civilised life has its certain disadvantages, one being a conditioning against awareness, a loss of the power of perception.

I wanted to say to the girl, 'Don't worry, it may never happen!' as a bus conductor once said to me in the days when I went about preoccupied with troubles. But I didn't, and she went by. After all, her reply could have been the same as mine had been – 'It has happened!' How isolated is a human being until that place in the universe, that warmth and strength within one's own being, is finally found.

About to flick Darkie's reins and suggest we move on, I became aware that the girl was returning on the other side of the street. She was looking at the cottages now, and hesitating, and suddenly she opened one of the gates and went in. She knocked several times, then came away and entered the next gate. Again there was no reply, and she went next door.

Such things are of great interest to the idle onlooker, so I allowed Darkie to browse a little longer.

The third door was opened almost at once to the girl's knock. Voices floated back to me.

'I'm demonstrating a new cleaning fluid,' the girl said, her voice bright and hopeful. 'May I show you? It's marvellous stuff. It'll take that mark off your door in no time.'

There was a large white splash that even from where I sat looked quite solid on the green door-post. She produced one of the bottles from her basket and sprayed it, applying a rag, gently at first and then in some desperation.

'They ol' birds,' said the elderly woman who had opened the door. 'I be always clearing up after them. You from the Council?'

'No, no,' said the girl. 'I represent the new wonder cleaner.' She was scrubbing harder. 'That ol' muck bin there long time,' remarked the other part of her audience. 'Proper ol' nuisances, they birds.'

The girl flourished her rag triumphantly. The mark had gone. She began to talk enthusiastically about the cleaning fluid, and I wondered if she would make a sale. But Darkie had lifted her head, so I took advantage of the opportunity to resume our journey.

It was half an hour later, when we had reached the top of the hill, that the rain came. At first a light silver spray, bead-

15

ing my hair and Darkie's mane. But the air was uneasy, and then the wind got up. Still Darkie was not disposed to hurry; her idea seemed to be, as so often in the field, to gain what shelter she could from the hedge.

I would not let her stand. Insistently I talked to her, and she took me across the road and on to the lane leading to the hill that drops to home.

And then it happened. A cloudburst, as sudden as a clap of thunder. Heads down, we crept close in to the little lay-by under the trees, which broke the straight fall of the rain upon us, and here I covered Darkie with the mackintosh sheet and put up my umbrella. Hunched beneath it, feeling like a gnome huddled under a toadstool while the skies emptied, I looked out upon the desolation of fields.

Yet anything but desolate in reality! However uninviting their aspect as the rain cloaked the countryside in grey, they were soaking up the refreshment that keeps them so brilliant a green. How restful to the eyes and the soul on a fair day. So English a green, like the fresh taste of an apple straight from the tree.

Of what did Darkie dream, with her ears at their resigned angle, as the cold rain tipped down off the leaves? A dry bed on her stable floor; her bowl of maize and carrots? I talked to her consolingly, and her ears answered. As I talked the rain eased. But it was still wet enough to remain where we were, and I was glad we did, little protection though the bank and the trees afforded, for a few moments later there was another downpour.

At the same time a girl on a bicycle came round the corner. As she caught the fresh onslaught of the rain she jumped off and threw the bicycle against the hedge, pressing in close herself. She looked familiar, but for the moment I could not place her, being more concerned that she wore no hat and only a short jacket over a summer frock.

'Come up in the cart,' I called. 'There's room for two. It's not bad here.'

She flashed me a smile and ran across. I opened the door and helped her up, and a gust of wind caught the umbrella and blew it inside out. I thought we had lost the use of it, but as I struggled to right it the wind caught it again and blew it back to its proper shape. We sat there helpless with laughter.

16

'Oh yes,' said the girl, as she crouched with me under the umbrella and I flung a wrap over her knees, 'you're almost snug here!'

'Well, at least it's not going down our necks,' I agreed. 'You must be nearly drowned.'

'Not really,' she said. 'I got over a gate and stood in a barn. Then I thought it was stopping so I started off again. Too optimistic, that's me.'

And then I realised where I had seen her before. She was the girl walking in the village street with a basket of bottles. I glanced at the bicycle and saw that the basket which looked as full of bottles as before, was strapped on the carrier.

'You need plenty of optimism for what you're doing, I expect,' I said, thinking at the same time that she had looked anything but optimistic in the village.

I mentioned that I had seen her in the village, and being all curiosity asked if the old lady whose door-post she had cleaned had bought from her.

She shook her head, and said with infectious good humour, 'You'll never guess what she said – *after* letting me tell her all about it.' She reproduced the voice so exactly that I couldn't help laughing.

'Pity reely. Better-Wear man come yes'd'y.'

She then revealed that this was her first time out with the bottles, and described to me how she had walked up and down the street as I had seen her doing.

'I was trying to pluck up the courage to start knocking at doors,' she said. 'You wouldn't believe the courage it takes to knock at your first door when you're selling something. I meant to go in the first gate I came to and then work down the whole row, but when I got there I just couldn't. I walked right by. Then I promised myself I'd knock on the seventh door down, but I was so bothered I lost count. Still, I made it in the end.'

'And was it as bad as you thought it would be?' I asked.

'No, not a bit. People are much nicer than you think. I had a sort of built-in fear of hostility, but nobody was hostile. Not today, anyway. Hope I'm just as lucky tomorrow – well, luckier really. I haven't sold anything yet.'

She told me she was spending three hours a day on the job, cycling to different villages and outlying farms.

'My mum's looking after the babies. I want to pick up a bit

of money for Christmas as my husband only gets a low wage, and to tell the truth I'm glad to get out and about. I don't like being stuck home all the time.'

I commented that it was rather a hilly district for cycling.

'Cars may be made for hills, but not donkeys and bicycles!' I said.

'Oh well,' said the girl, 'I can always push. And I expect your lovely donkey takes it a bit easy going up, doesn't she?'

I laughed. 'Yes, Darkie certainly takes it easy. The hedge is her snack bar, and she's always stopping for a bite and a rest.'

'I don't blame her,' said the girl. 'I often get off and have a lean over a gate. But I've always liked cycling.'

Her remark recalled to me the days when cycling had given me great pleasure too.

Glancing at the girl's modern light model, I remembered, too, the bicycle. Heavy and upright, it had nevertheless done a good many miles in its time, which was before the 1920s. London to Dorking and back had been a favourite ride. The roads had been quiet then, and it was I who had once drawn down upon me a rebuke for speeding.

I had enjoyed the sensation of skimming down a steep hill and was unable to take the bend at the bottom. Straight into a garden fence among the runner beans went I and the bicycle. The fence creaked and cracked ominously, giving way under the impact, but I remained still seated, gripping the handlebars, gazing through the green curtain of beans at a very red face peering back at me.

He was quite an old man, and was naturally very annoyed, though his first thought was not for his fence, but for me.

'Are you hurt?' Admittedly it was said in a tone that indicated I well deserved to be, and having ascertained I was not he pointed out with some satisfaction that I had torn my coat, and went on to upbraid me for the damage to the fence.

'Speeding!' he said accusingly. 'That's all you young ones think of nowadays. Speed. Dashing about on bicycles.'

I meekly gave him my address so that he might send on to me the bill for mending the fence, which in due course he did. Meantime I was more concerned about the bicycle, for I had damaged the front lamp, and told him I had to get back to London before lighting-up time.

Remembering those days, I understood exactly when the girl said, 'It's the thrill of the road. You know? Going somewhere, or – well, not really going anywhere. Just following the road. Guess I should have been a gipsy.'

She was sparkling and alive now that she had ceased to be preoccupied with selling her wonder cleaner, and I thought how one can never tell what another person is really like inside until they reveal a little of themselves at such a moment.

'I expect,' she said, 'you notice it with the donkey, don't you? You must enjoy it, travelling in a donkey cart!'

'Oh yes!' I said. 'I do!'

I would have liked to have gone on talking to her, but how difficult it is to express thoughts and feelings in ordinary conversation, even to a fellow traveller, and in any case the rain had stopped and she was climbing out of the cart saying, 'Well, thanks a lot for the shelter. I'll have to be going now.'

She was on her bicycle and waving goodbye to me before I even had time to ask the price of her wonder cleaner. Although I did not really want it, I had an urge to buy a

19

bottle if not too expensive for the pleasure of giving her a sale.

'Perhaps not a very good saleswoman, Darkie,' I said, glancing at the mud-splashed shafts, ideal for a demonstration. 'Or perhaps she was being kind.'

I hoped she would sell her bottles – maybe she would sell two for the one she had refrained from pushing upon me. I closed my umbrella, removed the mackintosh sheet from Darkie's back, and reflected that although the human race, in common with the animal kingdom, has always needed a certain amount of push for survival, it is pleasant sometimes to bask in an incident sheltered from the storm of continual striving.

With a flick of the reins we were on our way down the hill to home, Darkie's ears upright and her step sprightly. Home to a dry stable, to carrots, and a cup of tea (although she knew nothing of the coming brew-up in the kitchen, of course).

The journey had justified itself for interest again. And more than that. Stimulation had been given to my sleeping desire to take a longer journey in the donkey cart – to follow the road on and on in exploration and discovery, stopping here and there, meeting people I would not otherwise meet, seeing places new and having new life released within myself.

Yet surely it must remain a dream. I could see no way of working it out in practical terms. All the same I kept it in my mind. I said nothing to anybody, but just went on dreaming about what I began to call 'my donkey holiday'.

IT was about then that the weather began to settle comfortably into true summer again.

There were grasshoppers leaping in the tall grasses beyond the lawn, fragile acrobats swinging on stem tops, always that jump ahead of my shoe. The cats, too, were back in the long grass, having emerged from their wet day retreats in stable and hay shed, and the tops of cupboards indoors. They were lazily playing the grasshopper game, the little insects obviously intriguing them as they watched one grass blade vacated for another. A soft paw extended, a pat if they were quick enough, and the fascinating jump was repeated.

From the slightly giddy game of grasshoppers I turned my attention to the field. There was Darkie just about to take a roll on the patch of earth she and the goats have made for themselves in the grass. One hoof extended, she sent up an ecstatic little cloud of dust, blew through her nostrils, and then was over on her back – dry-cleaning her newly brushed coat! There she rolled, legs waving, watched by an admiring King Billy. He envies her this ability, and has attempted to copy, but his horns get in the way.

The goats have to content themselves with their slow, blissful rubbing along a fence, and this the mother goat was doing. The kid sat in the shade of the hawthorn tree, chewing. Beyond the bank the only shade in the next field came from the shadows of the grazing bullocks, and the flock of sheep sat together in the sun. The other occupant of this field, a beautiful brown horse, stood in statuesque contemplation of Darkie. For all his apparent dignity I have seen him roll, too.

I looked for the white rabbit in the garden. She was invisible except for the tips of her ears – deep down in her 'dahlia dig'. The dahlias grow at a crazy angle, but are as beautiful as ever, and Bettybunny loves the cool run she has made beneath them.

Yes, it was summer again. And again my days would slip into their pleasant summer pattern. Mornings, that first walk in the garden, as early as possible, to catch, if sleep has not defeated me, the freshness that is later lost in the golden warmth of the sun. Breakfast on the roof of the chalet for the birds. Even in summer there is always someone for breakfast. At that time it was chaffinches and young robins, the blackbirds and their broods having departed, and the tits too.

Their breakfast and Darkie's and mine, and Darkie's trip through the garden to the field. Bettybunny, in a compartment of the goat house, has had hers with the goats and is already in the garden enjoying, like me, the fragrance of the morning. She sits upright with nose twitching, tall ears a miniature of Darkie's.

And Susy? Her terrier nose is powdered with earth and her eyes are shining as she races up to me. She has been digging for moles again, and I say, 'Did you find the mole? Don't you hurt him!' which she understands exactly, and runs off, wagging, for fresh efforts. I don't follow because I'm fairly certain the mole will outwit her.

Before it grows hot I am busy on any small job required in the garden, or out on a short trip in the donkey cart. Afternoons are for resting in a comfortable chair. I sit on the veranda if not too hot, or perhaps on the horse-chestnut lawn, or in a nook of ferns and American currants, or on the tiniest lawn of all just outside the house where the periwinkles grow, or under the rowan tree on the big lawn. There are many places, each suited to an exact time of day, or certain weather. Tree shade is for a still afternoon, the veranda for a sun bath, the tiny lawn, walled and shrub-enclosed, for filtered sunshine and protection from a sudden wind that will so often flow in off the sea; and the fern nook is for complete privacy.

Then comes the evening, perhaps more varied in mood and activity than any other part of the day. Certainly it is a favourite time. So much has to be crammed into so short a time, yet it is also the part of the day to 'stand and stare', or, more accurately, to stand and *feel*.

Sometimes the flamboyancy of the sunset commands the long look, but it is the subtle change of light as the colours grow dimmer in the sky that I love most, the slow with-drawal of the day, when to stand and feel is the only thing to do out here in the open countryside where the coming of the dusk produces so spellbinding an atmosphere.

Yet I must not stand, for I am helping to make fresh beds for the goats, and my arms are full of straw. There are suppers to prepare of flaked maize, carrot, apple, and cabbage trimmings, three handfuls of hazel to gather as a tit-bit before the goat-house door is closed for the night. And for Darkie a last treat from the biscuit tin.

Presently there will be cat suppers, but it will be dark by then. Meantime Bettybunny has to be reminded that it is time for bed. She is no longer in the dahlia dig, but having a last nibble on the clover patch in the field. There is a goat to milk and a dog to take for a walk. So much to do before the approaching dusk blacks out the landscape, yet I have to pause now and then.

One moment is when the jackdaws fly over. All day they have been foraging on the further fields, and at evening they return to the woods – whole flocks of them flying over our garden, field and roof. A friendly company, breaking with happy chuckles into the delicate hush that has magically enclosed the countryside. Here is the time and place to melt away all mental sufferings, to minimise and even solve problems, to build up power for the journey through tomorrow.

How the jackdaws love these summer evenings. Then they fly low, a leisurely, almost dawdling flight, wings tossing in sudden dips and dives of play, and beneath the black cloud of them I stand and wait until they have all gone by, even the stragglers, who follow the main flock in smaller groups.

Their behaviour is closely linked with the weather. This happy, leisured flight home is only for the true 'old-fashioned' summer evening. Rain in the air, or wind, or chill, or later the shortening days and more swiftly approaching dusk will find them taking their homeward way more earnestly. Gone the play and happy chuckles. I look up and they are flying much higher. Sometimes their voices are completely silent, sometimes there is desultory chatter, sometimes a single call at intervals. Their speed varies too. I liken it from dawdling to swift walking pace to running. Whereas they took minutes to pass over before, they are then beyond the garden in seconds. Then this homeward flight is easy to miss if one is within doors when they come, and I am always sorry to miss it for the homeward flight of the jackdaws is part of the routine of the day.

But best are the summer evenings, when I stand with my arms full of straw and look and listen to my heart's content as they pass over. And when they have gone I am still held, for there is magnetism in the atmosphere at that hour. Who could not believe in fairies at such a moment? Certainly not I. For the fairies of childhood I would now substitute 'the unseen', for in the softly approaching dusk there is an enchantment and a peace upon the landscape that is un-questionably not of this world.

The dusk is luminous with flung light from the vanishing sunset and the first faint moonshine; to stand quite still in it is to feel as it were poised between the darkening earth and lighter sky, to be aware of soothing influences flowing into the core of one's being, so that the mind is at once and inexplicably freed from any pressure or problem that may be upon it as if the solution had already been arrived at. There must be other places, other moments, where such is possible, but it is in that moment in the Devon dusk that I imagine all the stress and strife in the world would be dis-solved away if, like me, the involved ones could stand within it and feel those harmonious rhythms gently vibrating in earth and air and their own being.

But to one who stands mesmerised a sudden summons back to this world can be almost alarming! To me it will often come as a stentorian bellow, resounding as a box on the ears. Of course it is that donkey at the field gate. I have dallied too long. Darkie is a spokeswoman for herself and the goats – and she can certainly use her voice! Once Freda told me she heard it half a mile away.

I go at once at a rush, and Eric mutters, 'No one bothers about me!' Good gracious, can it be *true*? I am aware of this instant attention given to the animals. I sometimes enjoy the luxury of breakfast in bed, and if it seems to arrive later than usual I will say, 'Late this morning!' And Freda answers as a matter of fact, 'Well, what do you expect! Six cats to feed, and the goats, *and your donkey*!'

My donkey . . . This is a standing joke. Mum's donkey! 'All right, Darkie, I'm coming!'

And so I entered upon the pattern of the summer days

when the weather changed that year, marvelling how quickly those days passed, even here where I enjoy the donkey pace of my old age. Soon autumn, then winter . . . and no more donkey driving until next year.

Again I was aware of that desire to *go further*. Afternoons I would dream about it as I watched the animals in the field through half closed eyes. The three goats sitting in a row steadily chewing, Darkie standing just behind, drowsy in the sun, not even her ears on sentinel duty.

Such afternoons are for dreaming, and on them I made wonderful journeys in the donkey cart. I needed no map, for I followed narrow lanes that wound their way westward, to Cornwall, pausing at field gates for Darkie's resting places while I brewed tea on a spirit stove and drank slowly, enjoying at each gate a different aspect of the view beyond the hedges. I saw the sun rise on these journeys in many a perfect place to frame it like a picture, and I saw it set beyond the evening fields or over the sea, and I waited for the stars to come out while Darkie browsed and browsed and browsed on new delicious verges and luxuriant hedges.

Through undiscovered villages we went – undiscovered previously by me – and every yard of every lane held the delight of unknown territory, every bend ahead promised the chance of adventure. We stayed nights at farmhouses and ate enormous breakfasts and scrumptious cream teas (at least I did), and Darkie bedded down with cows for neighbours.

They were delightful day-dreams. I planned our route, and ports of call, and imagined us arriving eventually at Land's End. I thought, too, of visiting places I knew as well as the unknown. There was the farm run by seven sisters, each with her allotted task in its management. Here in wet weather you could walk in the fields and meet cows wearing green coats over their backs. Walk in the woods and through the trees would appear a large pig snuffing for acorns – and how large pigs are, met in such circumstances! On these encounters I always waited behind the broadest tree trunk I could find until the pig had passed by.

There was the cottage where, on moving into the village from three hundred miles away, we were given tea – high tea. A table filled with plates of pasties, scones, Cornish splits, heavy cake and cream. We thought everyone was going to eat, but no, it was only for the two of us, the guests, and the

entire family sat around to watch us consume this feast. Even the most eager appetite would stumble a little, and under that interested gaze ours failed completely. It was not a meal I would care to repeat, but to drive up in the donkey cart and meet those friendly folk again would have been a pleasure.

I thought of the dignified old Cornishman who, in his eighties, still grew a garden full of vegetables and sold them in good measure for next to nothing to any neighbour who knocked on his door. And I would certainly call at the small snug house where lived the little London woman with the cheery voice – she who had survived the day she and her husband had retired to the country and she had sat and wept at the astonishing sight of her beautiful furniture being hoisted to the bedroom through a trap-door in the ceiling because it was too big for the stairs. But as the furniture accommodated itself to the house so did she to her new life, which, when I knew her, was filled with good turns for all and sundry.

Yet further on, and I would come to a rambling old house

where lived a widowed Cornishwoman who had befriended us, the only 'foreigners' in that village, and accompanied us to our first Furry Dance at which festivity, she said, it was the custom to wear a lily-of-the-valley in one's buttonhole. Our small front garden being entirely carpeted with lilies-of-the-valley this presented no difficulty, and on that bright May morning we felt as Cornish as the rest of the village as everyone merrily boarded the bus to town.

And so, in my dreams, the long journey by donkey cart went on and on – and was it this that was real, or the past, or only the sunny afternoon with the drowsy animals in the field and myself half asleep in the chair? There is a certain timelessness about such moments, and presently when I bestirred myself to some routine task I would feel I had broken the time barrier, and would feel both refreshed and free.

'Finished your library book?' asked Freda, on one of my dream journeys.

I opened my eyes to see the garden instead of the winding road, and confessed that I had not. 'I was miles away,' I said truthfully.

It occurred to me then that I would very much like to write about a donkey journey. The planning of the route, the preparations, the start, the adventuring from village to village, the little discoveries and excitements, the people I met, and finally the triumphant arrival at my destination after weeks – months? – on the road. It was then that the dream vanished like smoke up a chimney. I realised for the first time that such an arrival at some distant destination would be a weary rather than a triumphant one – and how would we return home? Simply turn round and repeat the journey in anti-climax, or incur some vast expense in getting ourselves transported back? The answer was, of course, that we would probably never arrive at all!

I, seated in the driving seat, might survive the weariness of a long journey, but I could never expect Darkie to go on walking day after day, nor insist that she pull the cart up and down so many hills. Hedge snacks and varied grazing would be no compensation for a worn out donkey miles from her own stable – she who likes nothing better than a familiar set routine each day. And if anything Cornish hills are even steeper than Devon ones.

Again I was transported back in memory, this time to that

distant summer day, bright with heat, when we took a train from Paddington and went to live for the first time beyond the Tamar. We arrived at five o'clock in the evening; the removal van was due at seven. But already a telegram had arrived. 'Regret breakdown. Arriving late.'

It was a pleasant wait, exploring the village, climbing a hill to find the old grey church with its door wide and the sunset glowing within, commanding, there on the summit, a view of the green wooded valley, brilliant in the evening light. What else but to step inside to say a silent 'Thank you'? We had come out of chaos to find peace – and what an unbelievable beginning!

Came night, and the village street, which had not a single lamp, was black. We groped our way back, feeling along the walls for we had no torch. Alone in the empty cottage, we waited. It was eleven o'clock before the street was suddenly swept with light, and the van with all our possessions climbed its last hill that day.

'Talk about hills!' said the removal men. 'We've never had to use bottom gear so much before.'

How friendly and cheerful they were as they told us all about the over-heated engine and the breakdown. They never complained, though they had had a long, hard day. All they unloaded that night were the beds. We slept upstairs; they slept downstairs on their own camp beds. One had a gun beside him – we were slightly alarmed! He hoped, he said, to get a rabbit or two on the way back.

Next morning, after everything had been unloaded, we stood at the gate and watched the big van slide gently away down the hill, its red tail light winking on the bend at the bottom before it finally disappeared from view. It had been like a farewell to old friends; we felt, I think, that they were going back all those miles to tread again our own familiar pavements, and with their going the last link had gone. In that moment the village was a strange land, and we the strangers within it. But not for long. Even if, as it is said, newcomers to a Cornish village remain 'foreigners' for ten years, this is not apparent on the surface, and we were made to feel at home from the beginning.

I thought now with nostalgia of this distant village, yet knew that my dream of driving there in the donkey cart could never come true. And with that thought I put aside all others of a journey beyond the boundary of a single day. Our own village, the woods, the beach – these must remain the routes.

It never occurred to me that I might still realise my dream of a longer donkey journey on a somewhat smaller scale than on the film set of my imagination. I would have been surprised to know how near I was to setting out.

I T was Matilda, the widowed mother cat, who began it. Widowed because from her young days, when she had come to us little more than a kitten, she had remained faithfully married (apart from one digression) to our tom cat, Marmaduke.

The digression had been an affair with a Siamese. This one litter excepted, all her kittens had our beautiful golden and white tom for their father.

Not that he was strictly 'ours', any more than Matilda herself – only the kittens, born within our boundaries, could be said to be our own, though even this is doubtful since their births were none of our choosing, any more than the advent of their father and mother had been.

Marmaduke was a Cornish cat. He appeared suddenly, from nowhere, at the second cottage we lived in after we had left town life behind as part of a forgotten past. There he was one evening at dusk, stalking among the evergreens – a large, powerful looking cat with a magnificent tail held high. Where he came from we never knew. He was not starving or neglected, but he remained in our vicinity and he cleared the plates of food we left for him in the garden. But he would not come near. The food was only eaten if no one was around. The sound of a door opening would send him fleeing like an easily scared nondescript puss instead of the noble looking cat he appeared to be when viewed from behind the curtains.

It took many plates of food to win even the slightest sign of trust from him – around one hundred and eighty of them to be exact, for it was six months before he allowed us to approach him. Soon after that he permitted himself to be stroked, though warily, but it took a year before he would cross the threshold of the house – except for one occasion when he was carried in.

He was a slightly battle-scarred tom, with small pieces missing from one ear and a nose that looked permanently scratched. On this occasion he had a bad wound around his eye. We took him in, and he understood that we meant him only kindness, for he remained submissive while we bathed and treated his wound. The healing of this wound did much to establish more satisfying relations between himself and us.

Before this, however, we thought we had solved the mystery of him. An advertisement in a local newspaper for a missing tom cat exactly fitted his description, though the address was a good few miles away. However, we telephoned immediately that evening, and it so happened that the missing cat's owner was on the point of driving to London and said that as he would be fairly near our village en route he would call to look at Marmaduke.

It was New Year's Eve. The time wore on, and we gave up expecting him. Then, just before ten o'clock, he came.

Fortunately it was Marmaduke's time for lingering in the garden, and the beam of the torch soon picked out his golden bulk.

'Ah yes,' said our visitor, 'a good specimen of a tom cat, but not mine, I'm afraid.'

He had had a cold drive, and only seconds had passed since his arrival. Politely we asked if he would like to come in for a few minutes. He came willingly, and as it was New Year's Eve we got out the ginger wine left from Christmas and sat with him round the crackling log fire, talking cats. After that I can't remember what we talked about, but we certainly talked, for he was a very pleasant, amiable person and made himself thoroughly comfortable in the armchair with his legs stretched to the fire, and it seemed quite agreeable to have an unexpected visitor. And so it was that we saw the New Year in – which we had not intended to do – in our own house with a complete stranger, for at half past eleven we all agreed that we might as well sit on for another half hour. So all the ginger wine went, and Marmaduke stayed, and at one o'clock our guest bestirred himself and said he really must be going as he had to drive to London. He was, he assured us, quite used to driving all night.

By the time we moved house again Marmaduke was part of the household, so he accompanied us. It was at this time, at the new cottage, that Matilda came. Hers was no secretive lurking and surreptitious licking of plates. She was civilised and sociable, and she took pains to make good friends with us in the time she spared from flirting with Marmaduke.

The subsequent litters of kittens have been another story, so suffice it to say that for three years it was a happy-ever-after life for Marmaduke and Matilda. Then change came to them both. After careful thought we could see no alternative to having Matilda spayed. Ironically, at the same time Marmaduke became ill with kidney trouble, and soon after her operation he died.

I believe she sensed his impending departure before we did. Just before she had her operation she changed completely. She, the most placid of cats, grew irritable with everyone, animals and humans alike, with the exception of Marmaduke, for whose sake she had come to live with us.

There was no comfort for her afterwards. She avoided the company of the young cats, insisted on sleeping alone, and no longer joined in the washing ritual. For a number of cats together love to wash each other. Her life otherwise became normal enough. She ate and walked and purred on a lap. But mating time came round again and she was yowling for Marmaduke. Finally she disappeared for two days and two nights, scaring us into the belief that something had happened to her. However, she returned on the third night looking exceedingly pleased with herself, and was soon talking her expectant mother talk, searching out cupboards for beds, and finally preparing an old coat by much kneading. Listening to her ecstatic purrs, we were saddened by the thought of her inevitable disillusionment.

She drifted from expectancy to indifference, but in a little while the yowling started again, followed by the disappearance. Again she came back, but this time she did not bother to make her bed. We were told that it was very unusual for a spayed female cat to seek a tom.

It was Matilda, therefore, who became the direct cause of my planning a journey. She had disappeared again, and this time a fortnight had gone by. We had seen her sharing an oak tree with a strange tom cat, and going each day to the rendezvous until she finally stayed away from home altogether.

'I must look for her,' Freda said. 'Something may have

happened. I'll ask at the farms in case she's gone over there.'

One afternoon she took Susy and walked along Matilda's known routes across the fields. A two-mile radius, taking in three farms. There was no sign of Matilda anywhere, and no one she spoke to had glimpsed a black and white cat who didn't belong.

We resolutely closed our minds to the obvious dangers – to snares set occasionally in hedges, to road accidents, to illness, to a fox at night. We held on to the belief that somewhere Matilda was safe and well, and would return in her own good time, reminding ourselves of remarkable cat stories we had read about cats who walked miles without mishap and appeared again long after they had left home.

It was not always easy. There were five cats constantly around the place yet there might have been none, for it was always the sixth we looked for whenever a door was pushed open, a gate climbed, or a small black figure glimpsed in the distance. And still she did not come.

Watching Darkie in the field, I reflected on the steadfastness of donkeys. No roaming instinct smouldered within that sober head; no desire to live other than in the pattern of days that life had set her. I took her a carrot.

'Dear old Darkie . . . so dependable . . . not like flighty Matilda . . . poor Matilda . . . poor, flighty Matilda . . .'

Then it came to me. The great idea.

'Darkie – you and I . . . *We* could look for her!'

Her ears were at their questioning angle.

'Don't you see,' I explained, making it sound as convincing as possible to myself. 'With you I can go further afield. A circular tour . . . all the outlying places . . .'

How long would it take? Within the restriction of a day we could only cover the same ground each time, so nothing would be gained. But give me a week . . . This, I decided, could be the journey I had longed to make. It could, in its way, be that donkey holiday I had dreamed about – but there would be nothing aimless about it. And what could be more satisfying than a journey with a purpose?

I could start immediately. That is, within a day or two, for there would have to be preparations. I would take one of those stoves they used for camping; a kettle, teapot. One cup, one plate, knife, fork, spoon, bread, butter, cheese, a few tins (not forgetting the tin opener) – the list ran merrily through my head. Apples and oranges. Carrots for Darkie. A bottle of squash. I would put up each day for bed and breakfast and at every farm I came to I would stop to look for Matilda among the cats . . . the innumerable cats that lived on and around the farms.

So narrow in memory is the distance between the present and the past when one grows older that I soon found my mind deserting the practical laying of plans for an excursion into reminiscence. Other summers, other holidays . . . and the best remembered of them all. The summer of 1914. A week at Southend in August. That fatal August when the world changed for ever.

It must have been very broad-minded of parents in those days to countenance a joint holiday for a boy and girl. Yet I cannot remember my mother raising any objection to my going away with Fred, with whom I had 'an understanding'. We did, however, stay in separate boarding houses, but in order to be together as much as possible we had no meals there. Prosaic for young lovers to meet for breakfast, yet in spite of it being the least romantic part of the day the prospect of meeting Fred at eight o'clock every morning for a whole week enchanted me. As soon as I was dressed I was out in the street. And there would be Fred coming towards me from his boarding house. We had enormous appetites, and romance had to wait while we went to a little restaurant to set ourselves up for the day with a hearty meal of bacon and eggs.

Looking back, I remembered a week of glorious sunshine, and myself sallying forth in white voile dress with a large sailor collar and frilled cuffs, and that dress reached to my ankles as they did in those days, despite the hot weather. I suppose I was cool enough. Certainly I wore a very large brimmed hat. There was no question of going to the seaside for a sun tan in those days. Nor did I bathe. We spent our days sitting decorously on the beach, going for walks, finding new restaurants for meals, and attending a show in the evening before returning to our respective boarding houses at the sober hour of ten.

On one occasion we went on a boat trip with a number of other people. Across the summers floated their gay voices – all singing in the light-hearted abandonment of a holiday mood. Even the songs I remembered; indeed the songs I

could not forget, in the light of what happened afterwards.

We were sailing along
On the Moonlight Bay,
You can hear the voices singing,
They seem to say,
You have stolen my heart,
Now don't go away,
Don't leave me, dear,
By the Moonlight Bay.

A commonplace enough little song, yet later it no doubt echoed poignantly to others in the boat that day besides myself.
And then we sang 'Never Mind'.

Though your heart may ache awhile
Never mind . . .

Never mind that into those sheltered days of our gently pedestrian lives was to come the collision of nations. We must, I suppose, have had some idea in the preceding weeks

35

of the threat to our security. There must have been some talk of the trouble in the world in the servants' quarters of the big houses where we worked. Yet it had seemed as remote from us as if we had lived in another world, though some instinct, perhaps, prompted us to take that first, and last, holiday together.

And so it was on the day after the boat trip, when everyone had been so carefree, that we heard war had been declared.

We sat on the beach looking out to sea, and Fred said, 'My poor old Bill's out there. I shall join up when we get back.'

His brother was already in the Navy, and his words were a vow I knew he would keep, although he was under age. Three months before his eighteenth birthday he was in the Army, one of so many eager youngsters who flocked to enlist in the spirit of patriotism.

Yes, it had been the holiday of a life-time, never to be repeated. Out of all the holidays I had ever had – the occasional weeks in the country near my childhood home in Dorking when I lived in London, those family fortnights at Ramsgate between the wars – only that week in 1914 remained clear. My memory was like a child's painting book, having a kind of crude charm in its packed pages of unfinished pictures, some pale and indistinct, some brilliant with mixtures of colour, with here and there a page that had stuck, and then, leafing over – *this*, as if a true master had borrowed the child's book and painted a miniature, perfect in every detail.

I tried to recall those other holidays, and fragments came back. Hayfields, a lighthouse, a lost handbag on a pier, beach donkeys . . . This brought me back to the garden, to an awareness of the field fence and Darkie looking over it. Good gracious, I now had a donkey of my own, and she and I were going to take a holiday together.

'Good idea, Darkie?'

She thrust her nose at me, ears aslant, and since I carried no tit-bit I assumed the gesture to mean that she shared my enthusiasm for the enterprise.

OF course there was opposition.

As I confided to Darkie, in the privacy of her stable one evening, all the best enterprises encounter this and survive it. She and I would overcome it, and go on our way as planned.

There is an irony about old age. One becomes as a child again, subject to the discipline of others' reasoning. I smiled a wry smile, remembering that I had once said, 'No, you *can't* go', and Freda the child had turned a chastened face away. Now Freda the mother had said to her mother the child, 'But you *can't*! You simply *can't*. A week's holiday travelling on your own with Darkie? Don't be ridiculous!'

'Darkie is a responsible donkey,' I pointed out. 'And I am a reasonably responsible donkey driver.'

She couldn't see the logic of this because saying 'No' was safer than saying 'Yes'. Her horizon was filled with road – a long road that I wanted to traverse alone (except for the donkey) for a week.

'Can you see anything wrong,' I asked Eric, 'in my taking a week's holiday with Darkie? A circular tour, just going a comfortable distance each day, and putting up for bed and breakfast.'

'Could be tricky finding a bed for the donkey,' he said.

I considered this, but decided that if I always stayed at a farmhouse they could almost certainly accommodate a donkey too.

'Where do you want to go?' asked Eric. 'I'll draw up a route for you.'

That, then, was the beginning of it.

I began to feel as if I was about to take off for America rather than setting out on a simple exploration of English country lanes. But then a seven-day journey by donkey was quite the most unusual holiday I had ever taken, and simple though it seemed I was soon up to my ears in preparations.

Freda had come round from her parental role to that of fellow conspirator when she realised my mind was made up. One does perhaps prefer to lay one's own plans, but when she fixed for me to telephone a neighbouring farm each day with what I can only describe as a progress report I had to agree. If she was going to spend the week in anxiety about me I might as well not go, and this was the alternative. She would call at the farm each day to check that I had telephoned – was still alive and donkey driving, in fact, instead of in need of rescue.

'Besides,' she said, as a little bit of bait, 'I can let you know if Matilda turns up, and then you won't have to bother with any more inquiries.'

I reflected that I would be very happy to know that Matilda had turned up, but would not cut short my tour if she did. Eric had prepared exactly the route I wanted, taking in outlying farms, villages, stretches of coast, downland and woods. It was a circular route, and we would do three to five miles a day. I could linger as much as I liked, and a day or two either way would not matter at all.

That is the beauty of donkey driving. You make no hard and fast rules either for yourself or the donkey. Instead you experience a great sense of freedom – freedom from care and freedom from pressures of every kind. If you do not get there today tomorrow will do. It is a relaxing creed, the creed of the tortoise, but it is also a tolerant creed and rivets the attention on an important truth (to me) in life – that the most important thing is to 'get there', wherever it is, no matter how you do it, and that to arrive slowly in your own time is better than not arriving at all. We all go through life in our own fashion, the hale and the weak, the handicapped, those who 'see' with their unseen eyes and those who do not. Many of us have goals, but different approaches. Some time or another we all 'arrive'.

I wished I could present the itinerary to Darkie for her seal of approval, pointing out that this lane would be deep between grassy banks to provide hedge snacks for donkeys, and that one was bordered by woods with trails of bramble and young hazel boughs; that here was a field in which she might rest for as long as she pleased and there a village where the summer visitors would receive her with undisguised admiration, as if they had never seen a donkey before (and perhaps some of them hadn't).

Of course, I did tell her all about it, and she listened in her sedate way as if it were real boardroom business, so to put a spark of joy in it I waved a carrot and sang to her, 'A holiday, Darkie! A holiday!', and she threw back her head and opened her mouth and bawled back at me. Probably about the carrot.

For one small person and one medium-sized donkey there seemed a great deal to pack. I set about it in a methodical way, listing everything I wanted to take. It included picnic equipment, Darkie's carrots and biscuits and week's ration of maize, to say nothing of her food bowl and bucket, so that I could get water for her. With great forethought I also included one mackintosh each; an umbrella; a spare pair of shoes, and various wraps. Thinking again, I added writing paper and pencils, and a few books. I resisted the idea of taking the transistor radio (if war broke out someone would be sure to tell me somewhere).

'What about your money?' asked Freda. 'Where are you going to put it? Don't give anyone a lift whatever you do.'

It didn't seem very likely that anyone would thumb a lift in a donkey cart, even for a nefarious purpose, but I was smiling for a different reason. Again the positions were reversed. It was I who had so often said, anxious about her on a two-mile walk home from school – there were no school buses in those days – 'Don't accept a lift from anyone.' Even at that time, forty-odd years ago, such admonitions to children were necessary, despite the impression these days that crime is a modern ailment of society.

In all the preoccupation with preparations I had almost forgotten about Matilda. I thought of her again the evening before Darkie and I began our journey as I walked around the garden and noticed the cats coming home, one by one, for supper. Five. Again the disturbing thoughts, the immense sadness. Even a sense of ridicule at my scheme to find her. Did one *ever* find a cat? They came and went as they pleased, and as Matilda had chosen not to come, or was for some reason unable to do so, my chances of finding her were small. Yet it was worth setting out on that tom cat trail around the farms. Where there were tom cats there could be Matilda.

But whether I would be fortunate enough to see her was another matter.

My pleasure in the 'holiday' was slightly dulled. Interesting though I hoped the journey would be, it was a quest rather than a holiday, and I knew that if it had not been for Matilda's disappearance I should not be making it. For that had been the incentive which had transformed my desire to travel further afield with Darkie into a definite plan.

I thought I would go to bed early, yet I walked again in the garden in the summer night. Stillness everywhere, a starlit stillness, as if not even a flower breathed, and into it at intervals came the strange night sounds, each sudden and solitary – fleeting sounds, making the stillness deeper. The half-hoot of a distant owl, the hoarse cough of a sheep, the eerie cries of some night bird I could not identify.

Setting the hurricane lamp on a path, I wandered among the trees at the end of the garden, and stood for a few minutes against the comfortable trunk of a fir. The trees were like a friendly community, grouped there under the night sky in all that expanse of field upon field beyond the garden.

Standing very still, I seemed to be received into that community and so to have its peace bestowed upon me.

Habit took me down the lane with the lamp. I did not really expect to see Matilda coming home as in the past, always the last of the cats to return for supper. I had so often met her. At the bottom of the lane I stood for a moment in my golden pool of light.

'Matilda,' I called softly, in case she should be coming over the field on the other side of the hedge. 'Matilda . . . ?'

But when the grasses stirred and faintly rustled it was only field mice. Matilda was not there. So I walked back up the lane with my lamp, suddenly tired, and knowing that I should sleep well.

I hastened to bed. Pillowed and blanketed, my last thought before sleeping was of Darkie, asleep now on her bed of straw.

Tomorrow she and I would be on the road.

I HAD intended an early start, but such things are not easy when you are older. Although I had asked to be called at a certain hour I was not called, and breakfast arrived on a tray.

'It's your last chance for a week,' observed Freda, making it sound as if I was to be absent for fifty-two of them. 'Better make the most of it. For all you know tomorrow morning you may be breakfasting under a hedge.'

'Nice prospect,' I said – without irony, for in theory at least such a prospect *was* attractive. The refreshment of early morning air, birds waking, the gentle warmth of sunrise . . . I remembered I had missed the weather forecast.

'Did you catch the weather?' I asked.

The weather . . . all the year round it is the predominating factor when you live in the country, especially when the living is done in rather more primitive conditions than is usual nowadays. It is of more importance to us to know if it is going to rain or blow or freeze than to know the date or even which day of the week it is. The routine of the days never varies, but the weather routine is like a theatrical performance. So we listen to every forecast on the radio unless we are interrupted or forget the time, and when we do it is a small disaster that dogs us through the following hours to the next forecast. 'I wonder if it *will* rain . . . I hope the animals don't have to come in early . . . the wind's getting up . . .'

'Did you catch the weather?' is one of our stock phrases, and despite the element of doubt in the question we would be surprised if the answer were 'No'. That morning I asked more anxiously than usual, for I did not want to hear that the outlook predicted any change in the settled warm weather we had been having for the last few days. Catch the weather indeed . . . yes, it would have been nice to rush out with a

42

large net and trap the sunshine and blue sky until my week's journey was over.

But I needn't have worried. 'A ridge of high pressure,' sighed Freda, who obviously would have preferred an approaching rain belt. But it would take an earthquake to deter me from going now.

I finally drove out in the donkey cart at eleven o'clock – but why worry about time? Since having Darkie I have learned to take little account of the clock. I keep donkey hours now, which means that while cultivating my time as profitably as possible I not only do it at a leisurely pace but aim at making my attitude to life in general as relaxed as possible.

'Mind how you go!'

That final cry of farewell – how often in the past had I used it myself, when I was the one to remain at home, deriving a comfort from the words as if they gave safe conduct. For it is never the one setting out on the adventure who needs them to be said. We adventurers are conscious only of joy in the morning and great things ahead of us. To the one remaining behind the world through which we go is fraught with danger, as if every car will run us down, or fellow travellers conspire against us, or we will in some way hurt ourselves. So we must wear about us the talisman of their protective words.

To mind how one goes in a donkey cart is not difficult – until a large man in a large lorry looms up in a narrow lane. I had chosen the narrow way to the village by way of change. We always went down the hill, the way of the traffic (when there is any), neglecting the slightly longer way round along the winding lane partly because it is longer and partly because if a tractor came along, or a car nipped out of the stream on the hill in the summer-time, to pass could be difficult. But now it was different. I was adventure-bound, so I went down the lane.

I saw the top of the lorry two bends away. Normally one cannot see what is coming along these lanes, with their bends and high banks, but the lorry's height revealed it. In vain I looked for the field gate on the left hand side where it would be possible to draw in. Then I remembered I had passed it. The lorry and the donkey cart were destined to meet in the narrowest part of the lane.

Car drivers were very friendly towards Darkie, and in awkward places will draw in and wait for her to pass, or even back to a wider passing place. I have had enormous lorries inch their way past the cart where it seemed impossible to pass, the driver leaning out with watchful eye on the side of the cart and a broad smile for the donkey. So I did not worry, but reined Darkie in before we drew any nearer to the bend.

Round it came the lorry, a metallic monster grinding to a sudden halt because its way was blocked by my humble conveyance. And I knew at once that this driver was not friendly. His impatient lorry had sounded angry, and his face matched it. We looked at each other.

As he leaned out of his cab to review the situation – though it was obvious that to pass was impossible – I said hopefully, 'I can't back her . . . ' It was such a *large* lorry . . . I couldn't very well say, 'Can't *you* go back?'

As it happened he had no intention of doing so.

'You can turn her round!' he said rather tartly.

For some reason Darkie opened her mouth and bawled. Speaking out of turn, perhaps, but I was rather pleased about it. It wasn't just *me* – there were two of us. Obligingly I climbed out of the cart.

Only once before had I known her 'answer back' to a stranger. Then she really had been in the wrong, but she wasn't admitting it. She had trespassed in an adjoining field, and the farmer had shouted to her to 'Get out of it!' No doubt feeling herself a cut above cattle, who are always ordered about by loud shouts, she had reacted to his peremptory treatment by running round him in a wide circle with head thrown back, trumpeting her disapproval.

If you want Darkie to do anything you have to ask her nicely, but farmers not being in the same category as car drivers and summer visitors, who all seem to think a donkey is someone special, she was hardly justified in expecting it on that occasion. To a farmer a donkey is 'stock'. Since our animals are more like individual members of the family we had to think twice when told, 'Keep your stock out of my field.' Could he mean Darkie and the goats, who all trespassed occasionally? He could and did. We pointed out that his sheep and bullocks also trespassed in our field. An amicable understanding was reached – *both* sides put up wire in the gaps.

The lorry driver, glowering as I talked gently to Darkie, was obviously in the farmer category.

It doesn't help to be glowered at when you are attempting to turn a donkey plus cart in a narrow lane. I knew what he was thinking all right, and any moment he might say it. Why didn't I get a stick and 'lace her about the stern works' as R. L. Stevenson so aptly put it. Not those precise words, perhaps, but something very like them.

While I was occupied with three things at once – trying to turn Darkie, talking to her, and rather ineffectually attempting to block my painful awareness of the lorry driver's presence and the unsaid words hovering in the air – I experienced the kind of rescue I thought only happened to pretty girls in old-fashioned films.

There came, walking briskly down the lane, a stout man with a stout walking stick. When he stopped beside me and raised the stick I thought for one dreadful moment that the lorry driver's desire was about to be realised. But he quite simply put the stick in the cart and with gentle firmness took the reins from me.

'Let me help you,' he said.

I was speechless; Darkie was speechless. Round she went neatly, the cart behind her. A smart manoeuvre, and she and the cart were on the other side of the road facing the way we had come. The stout man saluted the lorry driver, said to me, 'We'll be back,' and proceeded to lead Darkie up the lane. She hesitated briefly, but receiving encouragement from me and in her long life having learned never to oppose anything unnecessarily, was soon stepping out as briskly as the man leading her.

The lorry roared into life; I stepped back against the hedge to allow it to pass and promptly sat down in a tangle of bramble. Mind how you go! And here was I with thorns sticking in me, dispossessed of my donkey not fifteen minutes from home.

As the lorry passed me and crawled behind the donkey cart my view of Darkie was completely blocked. She in her wisdom had accepted the situation which had arisen, and was probably now anticipating a speedy return to her home field. Separated from her by the length of the lorry and a slowly increasing length of road, I knew a sudden fear. Suppose he was kidnapping her and would not stop to turn her back to me when the lane slightly widened. Already he had exercised a kind of Pied Piper mesmerism upon her. It was a foolish thought; I might just as well have adjusted my position in the hedge and waited comfortably for her return. But I didn't. I set off up the lane behind the lorry.

A car overtook me and slowed behind the lorry, then stopped. 'Hallo,' said the voice of an acquaintance. 'Where's the donkey then?'

'I'm afraid we've got separated,' I said, feeling quite foolish. 'She's up there.'

The car door slid invitingly open.

'Motor transport comes in useful sometimes,' said the smiling woman at the wheel.

I got in. Before I could explain we had drawn level with the donkey cart, now on the other side of the lane by the field gate, the stout man standing with Darkie as they waited to go back the way we had come.

'Ah,' said the stout man as I joined him. 'All change, eh?'

He winked at the car driver, helped me up into the cart and solemnly handed me the reins. I thanked him, he said it was a pleasure, and walked briskly on his way. The adventure was over, and Darkie and I resumed our journey peacefully and with no further distractions.

The midday sun was hot. We by-passed the village and rested on a green island between three lanes, Darkie tethered to the signpost (just in case she thought it was time to turn homeward from this unfamiliar place). I leisurely unpacked lunch for two. For her, flaked maize and carrots; for me, bread and cheese and an orange.

Beyond the hedge I could hear sheep cropping grass. Lark song drifted down out of the blue sky, and the sun seemed to drowse in its own warmth on the bank below the hedge. No traffic came along any of the three lanes, and Darkie and I, peaceful and alone on the island of grass, might have been on a real island in a tropical sea instead of there among the sleeping fields of summer. For indeed the world seemed very far away.

Others, no doubt, were picnicking at similar spots, enjoying the same sense of isolation and peace, the pace of life in the seventies forgotten for a spell. But at the roadside would

46

be the symbol of the age, presently to take them swiftly away from it. When I folded up my picnic paper and resumed my journey I would still be part of the slumbrous afternoon as my donkey dawdled on between the hedges. Although outward peace is conducive to that greatest of all treasures, peace within one's own mind and spirit, I reflected that the most fortunate of us must surely be those who have learned to preserve this inward state in all the circumstances of life.

'Yes, Darkie,' I said as I untethered her, 'we're going *on*!'

Her idea seemed to be that this was the moment to turn back to more familiar territory, but she responded willingly enough to my guidance in the direction that led away from home. What next, I wonder, said her ears at their upright angle. She was obviously all set for adventure. I was pleased, for it could have been that most disconcerting of all reactions, donkey resignation. But there is no doubt about it, Darkie is interested in new experiences.

We went along lanes between hedges as down a cloistered aisle, the sky our roof and no glimpse of what lay beyond the green boundaries. Then a gap, or a gate, and while Darkie had a rest and a snack of grass I sat back in the driving seat to enjoy the view that had suddenly opened out, a spread fan of country pictures with perhaps a curve of sloping fields, tree clusters, cattle on a skyline.

Then we came to thatched cottages, one with a garden full of roses. Roses that leaned over the porch, encircled the bedroom windows, tumbled in and out of arches, and topped the boundary wall. Here, conveniently, we waited for cows to pass, black and white and satin-skinned with health, buxom with milk, and mild and curious of face. A young boy and a dog were driving them, the dog busy and important, tongue lolling, tail waving, as it continuously raced alongside and then back again to the last cow in the procession.

The preoccupied dog paid us no attention, but the boy smiled to see the donkey. Then they were gone, and I had no further excuse to sit and look at the roses. Further along I dismounted from the cart to shoo a half-grown gosling from its bewildered wanderings back into the farmyard.

Then I thought of Matilda, and looping Darkie's reins over the gatepost I went to the door to start my inquiries. I went reluctantly, for it is a sad task, seeking a missing animal. It is not difficult to hope, even when hoping seems to have very little foundation; what I feared was the constant and almost inevitable drawing of blanks, which whittles away even hope and leaves so great a feeling of emptiness.

But there seemed to be no one home. I wandered round the yard; I found a barn and looked inside. This was a farm seemingly without cats. But of course it was not. They were somewhere around, in their own particular hiding places. For all I knew Matilda could have been among them. Disheartened, I went on my way.

When we came into a village I drew into the forecourt of the little general shop and post office, an idea having suddenly occurred to me. I was glad now that I had brought writing paper and pencil. I sat in the cart and wrote the following:

LOST. Matilda, a black and white cat. White from chin downwards, four white paws. Any information gratefully received.

I then added name and address, climbed out of the cart and secured Darkie, and went into the shop. A glance at the window had already assured me that advertisements were displayed. There was a washing machine for sale, a boy's bicycle wanted, kittens needing homes.

My advertisement handed over and paid for, a brief conversation about Matilda and the weather, and I was on my way again. As I left the shop a middle-aged woman with a weather-beaten face entered it. I had not gone many yards before I heard the ping of the shop's bell again, and a voice called, 'Just a minute!' And then, to clinch it, 'Whoa! Whoa, donkey!'

I reined Darkie in and glanced around, and there was the woman I had passed in the doorway coming towards me. She looked at me hesitantly.

'I'm not sure if I'm right,' she began. 'I acted on the spur of the moment like. But I saw your advertisement on the counter, and there is a cat, a black and white cat, straying round our farm. I don't know if it might be yours.'

In my eager response to this I jerked the reins, and Darkie started off again. The woman put her hand on the bridle.

'What a nice way of getting about,' she said. 'My, we used to do this years ago, but it's all different today, isn't it, with them motorways and such. Aren't you nervous in the traffic?'

We talked of donkeys, and then went back to cats again. She was vague about the exact markings of the stray cat on her farm, and said, 'You can come and look for yourself, but it's no use coming till after dark. It doesn't show itself till then. Usually it slips in to have supper with the others.'

This was too good an opportunity to miss, so I decided to call a halt. Explaining briefly about my tour, I asked if they did bed and breakfast at the farm. As they did not, she directed me to a cottage a few yards down the road, and then asked what I intended to do about the donkey.

For the first time I realised that there could be, as Eric had said, complications about getting Darkie bedded down for the night. One thing to make airy plans – quite another when they come down to earth level!

However, it turned out well. Not only was there a field at the farm available for her, but a barn in which she could sleep. As Darkie never sleeps in the open even in summer the shelter was important. I could not have imagined myself re-tiring to a comfortable bed leaving her in perplexity under the stars. Nor do I think she would have stood for it! Darkie never hesitates to ask for what she wants, or to voice objections if something does not meet with her approval. The quiet night air would most probably have been torn asunder by her protestations – strident tones not in the least resembling that placid description of a donkey's voice. Hee-haw indeed! No, I do not think anyone would have been able to sleep for miles around if Darkie had not been housed for the night.

We went to the farm first, and I took Darkie into the small, triangular green field complete with stream in which she was to be the only occupant. It seemed exactly suited to her, and as soon as she was unharnessed her nose went straight down to the grass and slowly and contentedly her peaceful hooves followed her exploring nose. I, also well content, left her there to call at the cottage.

Although we now have a place of our own which matches up to distant dreams, I still never fail to be fascinated by other cottages, other plots of earth. 'Oh, I'd like to live here' became a constantly recurring thought during that journey. My bed and breakfast cottage was just such a place. It was little and snug, with swallows under its eaves and a garden that bloomed right to its ancient doorposts, and it had one of those apple trees that lean down low, as the song says, and an old well holding pots of scarlet geraniums encircled by thickly plaited ivy.

The woman within was not, as I had expected, a cosy old body who had lived there all her life – or near enough – but a young woman. She had the most beautiful smiling dark eyes I have ever seen, with a quiet, almost shy manner as she showed me up a flight of white painted stairs to a little room that seemed to be tucked right in under the eaves, with a window almost at floor level, deep-set and wide-silled. A cushion there on a summer evening and one could enjoy the garden until darkness concealed it. I could have stayed there a month, and regretted that I had only one night.

My next task was to go out to the telephone to make my duty call to the farm near home so that Freda could pick up the message and learn that Darkie and I were still in one piece and enthusiastic about our journey. I decided against mentioning that with any luck I appeared to be on the trail of Matilda. It seemed to be too good to be true so early in my quest, and I thought it better to be sure before mentioning it. After this I visited Darkie in her field and she simply raised her head momentarily to make sure it was me and then went

on eating as if I didn't exist in her world at all. A sure indication that she had no desire to resume the journey that day.

Then I was free to do what I liked, so I thought I would walk by the sea. I went down on to the beach, among the family parties, the dogs, the beach balls, and the ice-cream, buying an ice myself and sitting on the edge of a jutting rock to eat it as I enjoyed the merry scene for a while. Too late in the day to indulge in a deck chair. Tea-time was approaching, and I was soon watching the slow but steady exodus from the beach as one little group after another packed their possessions together and straggled off with their folded chairs and overflowing string bags and their aura of happiness.

Soon I was nearly the only one left. Just a few children and walkers with dogs and the last family party on their way to the road. I suppose I must have looked lonely, sitting there on the edge of the rock, for a voice suddenly said, 'Beautiful evening, isn't it? Are you all on your own?'

And there was a Pekingese sniffing my shoes noisily and his sprightly owner, who looked not much younger than myself, looking at me over her spectacles.

'Oh no!' I said without thinking. 'I'm not on my own. There's the donkey.'

'*The donkey?*'

I shall never forget the way she looked around that empty beach, as if searching for another Pekingese. We walked up to the road together as I attempted to explain, but I don't think she believed a word I said for when we parted she said kindly, 'Well, dear, I daresay there will be donkeys on the beach tomorrow. I'll look out for you.'

'By this time tomorrow I shall be five miles further on,' I said, and hastened back to Darkie to make my first evening meal in a field, and bed her down for the night.

DARKIE was pleased to see me. Her eating was done for the day, except for the supper she would look to me to provide. Her upright ears, and the whole alert attention she was displaying to nothing in the empty field suggested her mind was already working on how she was to get it and whether her stable would suddenly appear quite magically in the middle of this unfamiliar place.

'All right, Darkie!' I called, and she honoured me for once by a direct approach although I held no hand extended with a tit-bit. At the same time she tilted her nose at me and bawled a short reproach.

'It's all *right*, Darkie,' I told her, and she followed me to the cart, where she stood in expectation of being harnessed. Oh well, if we did have to plod through the night to get home she was willing . . .

'No, no,' I told her soothingly. 'No more walking for you today. You're going to bed.'

I put flaked maize and carrots into her bowl and led her across to the barn. She will follow her bowl anywhere at any time, so there was no difficulty – in fact I didn't walk quickly enough for her and could hear her breathing right into my ear, after which I got little soft pushes on my shoulder from her nose.

At the door of the barn she hesitated briefly, viewing the interior. I placed the bowl on the ground and she went to it, and ate her supper as placidly as usual.

'Good girl,' I said. 'See you tomorrow.'

With this comforting farewell – and if she understands words at all she must know these, for I say them every night – I left her.

Picnicking is not always quite the same in practice as it is in the imagination. On my way back across the field to the

53

cart I was looking forward to a pleasant half hour of relaxation with a cup of tea, fresh cut sandwiches and a book on my knee. In actual fact it took the best part of that time to make the preparations.

The grass looked inviting and cushiony – or so I thought. It made my ground sheet look like a lumpy mattress, however, and testing it for comfort I found I should have to select my sitting place more carefully. The truth was I had done too much walking in my enthusiasm! Short distances, it is true, and level ground, but I had been to and fro quite a bit from the time I had left Darkie in the field, and what I was really after was a back rest and a convenient slope to the ground to rest my legs.

I eventually found it on the bank of the stream, against a tree trunk, and there I took the stove and necessary baggage, filling the kettle from my water container, and at last sat down contentedly to cut a loaf of bread. Balancing this on my knee I wondered why I hadn't brought a cut loaf. But this one had been crusty – lovely in the open air well spread with butter and wedged with cheese. The sandwich made, I set about making the tea.

By the time I was comfortably settled the tea was not as hot as I like it – still, it was tea. Cup in one hand and sandwich in the other, I decided to dispense with the idea of a book on my knee. After all, much better to listen to the bird song and watch the sunset. As it happened it was the tiny trickle of the stream I listened to, and the sunset had disappeared behind trees. A little chill crept into the field. Soon I was packing my things together.

I decided to take my bag to the cottage, and then as darkness came on make my way to the farm. I wondered if Matilda really would be there.

After a rest at the cottage it was getting dark when I reached the farm. I had not wanted to arrive too early, yet it seemed I had. There was no sign of either cats or supper dishes in the yard. As I hesitated a woman appeared and said, "T'idn't cats' supper for nuther half hour,' and disappeared again.

I went for a slow walk along the lane. A terrier came frisking up to me and insisted on making friends. Feeling slightly lonely, I was not averse to his overtures, and our acquaintance was progressing nicely when his owner came round the bend in the lane and shouted to him to get down.

'It's all right,' I assured her. 'I don't mind.'

'Oh, but it's not *like* him,' she said. 'He doesn't jump up at people as a rule.'

I remembered all the goodbyes that had been said – dog, cats, rabbit, goats. 'He can smell mine, I expect,' I said.

When he had finally been led firmly away I smiled to myself, recalling an occasion when Freda had rushed to the vet to collect medicine before he closed, and being in such a hurry had not stopped to change her clothes. She was wearing the slacks and sweater she wore around the place, looking after the animals, and that morning had received her usual caresses from King Billy when she took him to the field. He likes nothing better than to rub against her when given the chance, and keeping hold of his horns while he does so, she sometimes indulges him.

On arrival at the vet's she found the waiting-room crammed to overflowing. As she slipped unobtrusively among the crowd, attention was immediately drawn to her arrival by a large dog. Lying on the floor, nose between paws, he rose and strained to the end of his leash, fixing her with what

55

she described as 'an unbelieving stare'. Then he threw back his head and began to bark. He barked long, loud, angry, puzzled barks, and there was no stopping him.

'I think I was more embarrassed than his owner,' she confessed. 'It was a complete mystery to everybody except me, and of course I knew. I don't suppose he'd ever come across a human being smelling of billy goat before!'

There was a strong smell of honeysuckle in the lane. I wondered how many more scents I would have discovered if I had had a dog's nose. A fascinating subject.

The stars were coming out when I returned to the farm. Light streamed across the darkened yard from the kitchen door, which was flung wide open. The yard appeared empty, and I hesitated there where the light met the darkness as if I stood on the dividing line between the known and the unknown. I knew that cats would come into the yard! I didn't know if Matilda would be among them. When I went into the light I would know – soon enough. I reflected that sometimes it is necessary to be brave to know.

Through the open door came a girl carrying a large wooden tray loaded with saucers containing little piles of food. She placed the tray on a coal bunker and began putting the saucers about on the ground, at the same time crying in strident tones, 'Cats, cats, cats, cats, cats!'

As if the music of a Pied Piper had beguiled them, cats of all colours came streaking into the yard from various directions. Without any hesitation or difference of opinion each claimed a saucer. I found myself smiling. It was an astonishing sight, and I forgot about my anxiety although, as each came into the light, I could see that not one was Matilda. I had always imagined that our cats' supper-time – six of them – was something of a phenomenon, but it was a tea party to a banquet compared with this.

A woman came out – the woman I had seen at the post office. As she glanced around she saw me, and came over.

'That cat's not come yet,' she said. 'You wait, it'll be here directly.'

I now noticed the saucer set apart from the rest, nearer to the shadows. Again I was hoping, yet telling myself at the same time that it would be a miracle if the one who came was Matilda. We stood there without speaking, and within two or three minutes a stealthy figure appeared on the edge of the light. I could not see distinctly at first, but the sociable nature of Matilda was not in keeping with this display of caution. And then the saucer was claimed, the food attacked, and the light revealed that after all it was not Matilda who had come.

I felt a sense of loneliness as I went to spend the night at the cottage. Perhaps, after all, such journeys were not for me. The familiarity of home, the comfort of my own bed, the set routine with our own animals – why had I ever thought I had wanted anything different, even for a week? Out there in the strange dark lane, groping along to an unfamiliar bed, I felt as I imagined a lost cat would feel – yet Matilda was not *lost*. Either she was about her own affairs or some disaster had befallen her. As it was still impossible to tell which, I turned my thoughts to Darkie.

Was she, too, feeling strange and alone in her unaccustomed bed? I nearly went to visit her again before going back to the cottage, but I had already said, 'See you in the morning,' and now remembered that comfortable adaptability of hers to the circumstances in which she finds herself. Dear reliable old Darkie . . . I took comfort and courage from her example.

NEXT morning I awoke refreshed. I had slept well (even in a strange bed). So, apparently, had Darkie! She was alert and interested and quite willing for the road.

At the first opportunity I turned from the busier lane that led out of the little coastal village alive with summer visitors into a quiet by-way. These are always the routes for Darkie and me, and thanks to the map Eric had drawn so clearly I knew exactly which to take and at what point it would come out.

As I turned I saw an ice-cream van parked nearby with its colourful tail of sun-tanned children in their bright beach attire. A mite struggled past me so intent on keeping upright two dripping cornets in each hand, at the same time trying to catch the drips with her tongue, that she paid the donkey no attention. But all eyes in the little queue turned upon me, and I waved as the inevitable cry went up – 'Look, a donkey cart!'

As Darkie's quiet hooves wended their slow way between the hedges I was, as so often when out with her, transported in quite a different way. Back into the past. Now I found myself in the world of seventy-odd years ago and remembering, of all things, ice-cream! How we used to bring it home fresh made from the dairy. I have never tasted ice-cream like that since.

No longer an old woman holding a donkey's reins, I felt all the jubilation of youth and vigour as I walked and skipped and ran from my home in Marpitt Hill, Edenbridge, down to the shop to buy butter. The order was neatly on my tongue as my mother had impressed it upon me – 'Half of fresh butter and a quarter of salt, please.' We called unsalted butter fresh butter in those days. The fresh was for my mother, little brother Victor and me, but my father preferred

the salted. For this purchase I paid tenpence (not ten pence – two shillings – but ten good old-fashioned pennies!). Fresh butter was one and twopence a pound, and salted one shilling.

Years later I remember going into a shop and asking for half a pound of fresh butter. I received a blank look from the assistant, who glanced at his display in some bewilderment. The astonishing reply bewildered me in my turn – 'The freshest we've got is from New Zealand!' I soon realised that he had been born long after my time, and hastened to explain that what I actually wanted was unsalted butter.

I cannot remember why I always had to make the half-hour walk to the shop for butter when I was a child, for we lived alongside a shop that sold groceries. The two men who ran it lodged in the house, and my mother provided them with meals.

Once again I was back there, playing in that paradise of a garden between ten-foot walls...a garden filled with fruit trees. I was gathering windfall apples, gazing up at the pears, longing for them to ripen into their juicy lusciousness, picking a Victoria plum that nestled warm in my hand from the sun as I ran off to school, and yet again asking my mother with great longing, 'When will the little plums be ready?'

The 'little plums' as I called them were damsons, and

59

from that time a favourite of mine, stewed and eaten cold. There were also peaches in that garden, ripening to the rosiest of blushes against the weathered walls in the hot summers of those days.

But the house was not our own. Like all working people at that time we were renting, and when the shop attached to it changed hands we had to move. It was goodbye to the lovely garden when we moved down the hill to Sunnyside alongside the railway. How easily the names come back to me! We lived in various houses when I was a child, as it was quite easy to move at any time then and my father's work necessitated it, and I can even remember the house numbers.

I drifted out of my day-dream that morning to find that Darkie, as always happens on these occasions, had stopped to do some dreaming of her own. There she stood, even her ears looking lazy, and not until she heard my voice would she amble on again.

After that we had several breaks while I called at farms in my search for Matilda. It seemed that no one had noticed a cat around who didn't belong, but on such a lovely morning I refused to be disheartened so early on my journey.

We had now emerged from our narrow lane, crossed a road during a lull in the whizzing cars, and were once more on a quiet road leading out to the hillocky expanse of the burrows with the sea beyond. This was not strictly an essential part of our journey as far as the search for Matilda was concerned, but I had not been able to resist including it.

Now we were making our peaceful way by a wide, gently flowing stream on which white ducks were swimming, looking as leisurely as ourselves. The road ahead stretched flat and straight. New territory indeed! I felt I had entered another county after the twisty, hilly lanes to which we were accustomed. With the water flowing beside us, and the level fields, a completely different atmosphere seemed to enclose me. I began to feel now that I was truly adventuring. Timelessness is always a feature of our journeys, Darkie's and mine, but never more so than along that road, for I was aware not merely of my freedom from the clock that day but of the ancientness of that place conveying itself to me at every step Darkie took, and into this old but ageless place

60

with its air of complete remoteness I and the donkey and the ducks came as mere passers-by.

On to what enchanted ground had I strayed? Eating my lunch against a stone wall I noticed further along the wall a large black bird observing me. It was a young rook, and at first I thought it was unable to fly. But it flew a little, and settled on the wall again nearer to where I was sitting. A thrown crumb was observed by one cocked eye, but no attempt was made to take advantage of this unexpected manna from heaven. Could it not feed itself? I glanced about for a parent bird, but it seemed this solitary one represented all the bird life there.

Presently I got up and offered the crumb to the bird. It did not fly, but to my amazement allowed me to stroke it, then to pick it up. I perched it on my wrist and it appeared to enjoy being gently stroked. Then it flew off leisurely and disappeared, and Darkie and I resumed our journey, I indulging in fanciful notions derived from half-forgotten fairy tales, she following her nose in her own dreamy way.

I tethered her where brambles had multiplied and formed a high green pinnacle covered with a liberal harvest of ripe blackberries, all shining in the sun. Feeling as free and easy as a gipsy, I ate my dessert from these bushes, then wandered a short distance over the grass, wishing I had the energy to follow the devious paths that led up and down the hillocks. They left the imagination as breathless in anticipating the delights of all those invisible hollows ahead, as the physical exertion of adventuring among them would have left a body as advanced in years as mine.

So soft and cushiony was the grass into which my feet sank that I couldn't resist a desire to sit down. Near me was an exquisite patch of tiny yellow flowers, and while idly wondering what they were, and going over the names of flowers in my mind, I was suddenly reminded of my Aunt Polly and her eight daughters. Each one of those little girls was given a flower name.

I remembered them all – May, Rose, Iris, Lily, Violet, Marguerite, Marigold, Poppy.

With the expected arrival of a ninth child my aunt's choice among flower names which were also girls' names had considerably narrowed. Her problem was solved by the unpredictable – after eight girls, a boy! While I was trying to remember what she called him I must have dozed off on that comfortable grass in the sun, for my thoughts transported me into a lovely dream of long-ago childhood, and I found myself playing with my eight cousins, all of whom seemed to be dressed in the petals of the flower they had been named after.

We were playing 'Sheep, sheep, come home.' It was played by two groups of children with another child to play the wolf. It went like this:

'Sheep, sheep, come home.'

'We can't, the wolf is coming.'

'The wolf has gone to Devonshire and won't be back for seven years. Sheep, sheep, come home.'

And so it went on, resulting in sheep fleeing from the wolf, but in the way of dreams instead of reaching that stage of the game it was I who was in Devonshire, not in the guise of a wolf but as my present-day self, hurriedly rounding up the cats and the white rabbit as the hunt came up the lane. They were all there but Matilda, and I couldn't find her anywhere, though there I was, searching under bushes and even climbing trees!

At that moment I opened my eyes to an unexpected sight, which I thought for the moment was an extension of the dream. Opposite to me across the hollow sat a woman knitting. A few yards away an elderly man was kneeling on the ground, head bent in an engrossed fashion. He seemed to have some sort of net spread, and held a magnifying glass in one hand.

I closed my eyes again, expecting the pair to have disappeared next time I opened them. But these two were real enough, and as I wakened to full consciousness the woman looked across and smiled, then gathered up her knitting and sat down closer to me, looking all set for a sociable chat as she remarked, 'We didn't disturb you, did we? My husband's hobby is entomology, and he's on the trail of something or other as usual.'

Her husband took not the slightest notice, still being intent upon the patch of ground. I assured her that they hadn't disturbed me, and glancing to see that Darkie was still happily occupied in browsing decided to enjoy a few minutes' conversation before she and I resumed our journey.

It proved to be the most fascinating conversation I had on that journey – indeed, the most fascinating for many a long day.

LIKE all conversations when I am out it began with Darkie. It then progressed quite naturally to Matilda and so to all the other cats, the white rabbit, the goats, and Susy. My companion showed such great interest that I was soon asking her, 'Have you any animals?'

To my surprise it was some moments before she answered. Then she said somewhat hesitantly, 'I used to have a dog.'

I guessed then that having lost her dog she had not cared to replace it, so I changed the subject. Perhaps it had happened not so long ago. I began to talk of anything – the weather, I think, and the summers of long ago that I remember so well.

She was in her fifties I would imagine, so she could not remember as far back as I could, and she took a great interest in my account of life in the early days of the century. Then she asked what I thought was the greatest difference between then and now.

To me the answer was simple. I had thought about this so often on my quiet journeys with Darkie, reminiscent of days gone by.

'Everything felt so secure in those days,' I said. 'Even the world seemed much smaller and snugger. Of course, I know there has to be progress . . . '

'Progress?' She smiled. 'Perhaps it's more important where one's progressing *to*.'

We talked then of the delusion of security, and were happy to find that in the course of our lives we had each made the same discovery – that real security is an inward state. The walls may tumble, but *here am I* . . .

It happens sometimes. One meets a stranger with whom one is in tune. She sensed this, too, I think, for she was suddenly asking, 'Have you ever had any psychic experience?'

64

I realised she was not asking me to recount any such experience, only to express an awareness so that she herself might continue the subject, and I was glad of his. The question was unexpected, and I was not prepared immediately to delve into that secret compartment of my mind where personal treasures are stored. I simply said, 'Yes, I have ... occasionally.'

There was a pause, and then she said, 'More than once? It only happened to me *once*. But I'm not really a psychic person.'

'Well,' I said, 'neither am I. Whatever a psychic person is. Aren't we *all* – underneath? I think of it as a window in the mind. Sometimes open, sometimes closed.'

She had ceased to knit. The busy needles lay idle on her lap, and she gazed down at them as she began her story.

I listened with considerable interest, and was not exactly surprised when it turned out to be about the dog she had once had. It was, she said, a Labrador retriever, one cross. They bought him at the age of eight weeks, just after the war, as a pet for their young son. Her first memory of him was of this tiny black pup scrambling across the floor of a garden shed with half a dozen others, extricating himself from them and going straight up to her. To clinch the deal he sat on her shoe and pawed her leg.

It was, she said, the only friendly overture he ever made to anyone who tried to become acquainted with him, for from the moment they bought him he became a one-family dog. He demonstrated this the following day when she handed him over the garden fence to an admiring neighbour – his squeals were so anguished that no amount of petting would quieten him until he was handed back again. The following week he had gained confidence, securely riding in his mistress' arms when she went into a shop. The semi-circle of assistants who gathered to pay court to him were astonished by his reaction. As soon as a finger was outstretched to stroke his diminutive nose he gave a very plain answer – a growl, she told me proudly, deep in his throat, and he just two months old.

She said he had the prettiest face and never grew very large, being cross-bred. His good looks always drew him attention, but he would never respond to it. Always he drew back from an outstretched hand, answering flattering words with a growl or a bark, and refusing to allow himself to be touched. He behaved in exactly the same way with people who came to the house regularly, and to her knowledge no one but themselves ever stroked him.

His devotion was two-edged. If he did not want attention from other people, neither should his owners give it to other dogs or, indeed, accept any advance from them. On walks other friendly, raised noses and waving tails had to be rigidly ignored, otherwise all hell broke out. He never attacked these dogs, but created a tremendous commotion, which was better avoided.

At that time, she said, her mother was living in the house, so he was never alone in it. Later they discovered it was fatal to leave him alone. He would howl for hours, disturbing all the neighbours. Over the years his faithful, friendly companionship came to mean a great deal to them. Once, rather than leave him alone in the house, they took him at two o'clock in the morning to a hospital where their son was very ill. They took it in turns to sit at their son's bedside, the other staying in the porter's lodge at the gate, the dog being permitted to go no further. She spoke gratefully of that porter, and the cheerful fire he stoked up for them.

When the dog was nine years old he developed kidney trouble. Until then they had taken it absolutely for granted that he would live to a good dog's age of fifteen or so. His death, she said, was like losing a child.

Some weeks after the dog's death she had gone on a shopping expedition to a distant town, taking sandwiches with her. At lunch-time she went into a park to eat them. It was a spring day, very bright and fresh, and she walked over to an expanse of grass and sat down on one of the seats.

She had not been there very long before a lean, rather bedraggled dog came up, sitting at her feet, tongue lolling. He looked at the paper bag containing the sandwiches with longing eyes. At first she ignored him, but all the time she was painfully aware of the hungry look about him. Eventually, and somewhat gingerly, she threw him half a sandwich. He devoured this and returned for more.

She continued to throw pieces in a detached way, conscious of a deep desire to be loyal to the dog she had lost without being unkind to this one. She even made a little resolve that when she got up to go she wouldn't so much as

66

speak to him, much less stroke him.

The dog, however, had different ideas. When he realised there was no more to eat he became consumed with a desire to express his gratitude for the brief meal. The expectant attitude gave way to exuberance. He jumped up, tried to lick her hands.

'No,' she said. 'No. Go away.'

She got up hastily and collected her things from the seat. All the time the dog was leaping round her. She could think now only of her own dog, and wanted nothing more to do with him. But suddenly he grabbed a handkerchief that was slightly protruding from her pocket.

He stood there, handkerchief in mouth, tail waving, eyes bright with fun and the desire for a game. Why on earth she didn't ignore him and walk away, leaving the handkerchief, she would never know. It was the obvious thing to do, she said, but instead of that the one thought in her mind was to get the handkerchief back.

She demanded that he gave it to her.

He edged away, always a few steps out of reach, every

time she approached him. Almost without her realising it several minutes went by like this. Then he was dancing round her again, tossing up the handkerchief and catching it, scrambling it between his paws, darting off and back again, and in spite of herself she was joining in and giving chase.

To an onlooker it would have looked like a high-spirited game played by dog and owner. She lost all count of time, but ten minutes at least must have gone by. Then she caught the dog, held his collar, stroked him, and coaxed him to give up the handkerchief. He submitted and licked her hand, then realising the game was over bounded off across the park.

She went on her way, vaguely unhappy. Back in the town again she forgot the whole incident as she finished her shopping.

When she got home she didn't even remember to tell her husband about it, though she was in the habit of recounting little things like that. She got the evening meal and sat down with him at the table.

As she sat down, she said, a strange thing happened. For a moment she seemed to be held in a kind of immobility so that she was actually incapable of moving. It was like having one's mouth frozen at the dentist's, only it affected her whole body. Simultaneously there was a violent sensation of scratching in her lap.

In a dazed way she said, 'There's something in my lap. There's a mouse in my lap . . . ' It was ridiculous, she told me, but the only thing she could think of was a mouse, and she was not convinced of that. She was aware that her voice sounded strange – a long way off.

Her husband bent down on his side of the table and at the same moment movement came back to her, and she lifted the tablecloth. Her lap was empty. There was nothing to be seen. They continued the meal, and the incident was not discussed.

As she reached this point I, of course, was thinking of the dog she had lost, and I thought this was the end of the story – that she would tell me how she suddenly realised the incident in the park had in some strange way caused her own dog to return and draw attention to its presence. But there was more to come.

In the middle of the night she half awoke to find that her right hand was groping about the bed, seemingly of its own accord, feeling over every part of the bed within reach, as if searching for something. She felt the heaviness from a deep sleep still upon her, and seemed quite unable to control the movement of her hand. It just went on groping, and as it did so she became aware of a strong conviction that there was something in the bed she had to find. She had no idea what it was, and being very tired was soon fast asleep again.

Later she woke once more – how long afterwards she had no means of telling. But this time she was wide awake in an instant, all her senses alert. She was aware of what she described as 'a terrible commotion under the mattress.' She was petrified. The first thought that came to her mind was that the mattress was alive with rats.

Almost immediately her husband woke, demanding sleepily, 'What's the matter? What are you doing?' She couldn't remember what she answered, but for a few moments they both lay listening. Then the noise ceased.

In the morning the night's events were still very vivid in her mind. When she went to make the bed she determined to search thoroughly. She didn't know what she expected to find – in fact, she didn't expect to find anything. It was simply a task she had to do to satisfy herself there was nothing there.

Methodically, she stripped the bed completely, removing all the clothes and pillows to a chair. She then took the mattress cover off carefully. As she did so she noticed a small object in the very centre of the mattress. When she picked it up she had no idea what it was about to convey to her.

She stood there, she said, with this tiny thing in the palm of her hand, staring at it in puzzled disbelief. How *could* it have got there – why should she find it *now*, after the strange events of the night? Her puzzlement and her disbelief both melted away, and she described to me how she stood there with the tears welling to her eyes until her vision was so blurred she could no longer distinguish the thing she held. When she sat down later to examine it she saw she had made no mistake.

At this point she looked at me and reached for her handbag. 'I must show you,' she said. 'I carry it with me everywhere.' She took out a small box and opened it.

There in the palm of her hand lay a small black object. She gave it to me and I examined it. Unmistakably it was

69

a dog's cast off nail, slightly hollow at the chunky end where it had broken off.

We both sat there looking at it while she said, 'I've never told anyone before except my husband. He believes in what happened that night – he believes the dog came back after the incident in the park, but he doesn't believe he caused this nail to appear. He thinks that somehow it got on to the mattress during his life-time, and what happened in the night was to draw attention to it.'

Her sincerity was beyond doubt. I couldn't resist asking, 'And what do you believe?'

To which she replied quite simply, 'I don't believe. I know.'

Returning the nail to the box and the box to her handbag she said, 'After all, I'm the one who makes the bed. And I'd only turned the mattress two days before and shaken the cover.'

I pondered the significance of this, and again being convinced of her sincerity could only marvel at the phenomenon. Yet why? I asked myself. Why should it seem so remarkable? Surely it is only because it is outside our experience. Was not every created thing remarkable? Even a tree? If we had never seen a tree before, and we looked at it with all our eyes, all our being, instead of as we usually look at things, not really seeing them, wouldn't that tree seem a most remarkable thing?

She asked me my opinion of her story, and I replied along the lines I had been thinking.

Her smile was grateful. 'I'm sure you're right,' she said.

After that there was really no more to be said. I became aware of how much time must have passed as I sat there unconscious of it, listening to her story, and quietly took my leave. I thanked her for telling me the story, for I counted it quite a privilege to have been told it. And then it occurred to me to ask her if she would mind if I wrote about it some time in the future as it was so worth sharing. Her reply was, 'Please do. I've often thought I would like to share it.'

As I climbed into the donkey cart I was aware of her husband still busy on his hands and knees on the grass, and I heard her knitting needles already clicking again.

The wheels turned slowly behind Darkie's slow hooves, and with the reins slack in my hands I was back to my dreaming and my memories. This time, with the story I had heard still vivid in my mind, they took a new route, and as we went sedately on through the quiet afternoon I was unconscious of time again. Not until I became aware of a different slant to the sun's rays across the fields did I realise just how long I had lingered back on the burrows.

I now had no hope of reaching my next destination before sunset.

'DARKIE,' I said, 'what on earth shall we do?'

The question was not one to which I expected an answer – it just helped me to say it, to get the sudden panic in my system out of it, into the open. To share it, even with a donkey, and so in expressing it to clear the path to practicality again.

As I might have expected, though, Darkie answered. She stopped. One ear up, one down. She did not eat. She simply waited.

'All very well, Darkie,' I said, 'but we can't spend the night here now, can we?'

Or could we? Camping out in an emergency had certainly crossed my mind during those delightful days of planning this expedition. How possible it had seemed then, how easy; what infinite charm the idea had held! Now that such a situation could suddenly be upon me I saw it in quite a different light. I would be cold, damp, cramped, stiff and generally uncomfortable. I might even know what real loneliness felt like in the long hours before dawn. To be alone is not to be lonely, to be in the company of a donkey is to have the most perfect companionship, but to lie sleepless in the middle of nowhere simply sensing that rotund hulk of her somewhere in the vicinity, not even an ear tip visible, aware only of the night all around, that intense, alive outdoor blackness that is like a presence in itself when the moon has gone – this, to me, would be loneliness.

Of course, I could combat it. The outside must always give way to the within. I reminded myself that it is within that we live, experience all our sorrows and joys. Outside is just the scenery; the events in the midst of it all are the enacted drama we temporarily take part in. But within ourselves is our door to reality. A single thought can be the door, I realised at that moment, and we are over the threshold between the two worlds – the outer world of the eyes and the inner world of the mind. Unbidden came lines I had once read in a quotation from a poem by Rauschenbusch. 'In a moment, in a turning of a thought, I am where God is.' Surely no one could doubt this once having found their inner harmony, been wrapped and lulled and cradled in that mysterious state of peace which has no connection at all with whatever may be happening outside oneself.

Yes, I could lie in the night alone and find peace, but perhaps it would not be very wise of me when my limbs demanded a bed and Darkie a shelter. So we would go on and take our chance, since we could not reach our intended destination.

'On, Darkie,' I said, jerking the reins. 'On we go.'

And on she went, ears high.

It was worth going on to see the lapwings. Down the sky they came, so that the whole upper air seemed filled with them. They wheeled and turned and rose to heights of sky as if flying for the pure pleasure of it. I counted twenty . . . fifty . . . a hundred. At two hundred I stopped, for there were still more.

As dusk approached we snuggled along a lane between high hedges, so narrow here and off the beaten track that I was fairly confident of being the only vehicle. But soon, I knew, it would be necessary to light the lamps, for although I had never had any intention of travelling after sunset they had fortunately been packed in the cart in case they were needed.

How to keep up ones spirits when circumstances press upon them? In my young days we always sang. In fact, in our family we were always singing, not only to give a lift to

73

our spirits, but as an expression of happiness and often as recreation. No radio or television to switch on in those days. We were both performers and audience, and what immense satisfaction we found in it, singing to suit our mood. We would quite literally 'sing for joy', and equally in sadness as we sought for strength, to give ourselves courage in hard times, or even simply to relieve tedium.

I can remember my mother singing as she whitened the door-step with hearthstone, and polished the brass door knobs till they shone. As often as not the song would be 'Gates of the West', which I remember her telling me she once sang as a solo at a concert in the Albert Hall in London. I wished now I had asked her more about it, for I don't know what concert it was or how she came to be singing there.

My father, coming in from work, would sing as he washed himself at the kitchen sink, his favourite song being 'Over the burning plains of Egypt', all about 'a lad in the Scotch Brigade'. At one period my little brother had a favourite hymn he was always singing, 'There is a book who runs may read'. Alas, his perception at that time was more advanced than mine. I was scornful about this hymn, perhaps because he annoyed me by constantly singing it, and I would say scathingly, 'How can you read when you're running?' Yet today how eagerly do I 'read' that book – the 'book' of Nature – which he understood long before the age of twelve, when he died.

I used to sing with the Young Helpers' Choir, who gave concerts at the local Workhouse, and one day, like my mother, I had my hour of glory. Unlike her I was not a soloist, but one of five thousand voices when choirs from all over the country gathered in London to sing at the Crystal Palace.

What a thrill that had been! I recalled it vividly in the twilight of that summer evening as Darkie and I made our way along the narrow lane. There was the unusual excitement of a train journey, which in the ordinary way we had no occasion to make. The only other train journey I can remember making in my early childhood was once when we moved house. The train took not only ourselves but all our furniture and possessions as well.

To my mother fell the task of packing everything – and

labelling it too. Every single article, from the kitchen table to the poker, had to have our name and address securely attached to it. My father was already in another village, having been transferred there because of his work. He had secured us a rented cottage, and was on the platform to meet us when the train arrived. Was it over seventy years ago, or yesterday? It seemed yesterday as I saw myself stepping carefully out of the train, restraining my joy at seeing my father again as I concentrated on keeping the bird cage I carried as steady as possible so as not to upset the canary.

The journey to sing in London, though, was the longest I had made. We were living at that time in East Grinstead in Sussex. For many of the children it was their first time in a train and everyone was bubbling over with high spirits. Some of the mothers and younger children came too, but we choir girls were easily distinguished as we all wore cream dresses with red bands shoulder-wise across them bearing the embroidered letters in white, Y.H.C.

My mother and young brother Victor came with me in the train, but once having seen me safely at the Crystal Palace with the others they took their departure. 'Aren't you going to stay and hear us sing?' I remember asking in some disappointment. But a journey to London was an event even to my mother, and she had plans of her own. I was told to be good as she was going to see my Aunt Clara, where she would be staying the night, and my father would meet me on East Grinstead station when I returned.

I soon abandoned myself to the exciting happiness of it all. We had tea, and after the singing there were fireworks. When I finally arrived back at midnight I was almost too sleepy to savour any more joys, even that of being up to so late an hour and walking home in the night hand in hand with my father.

Now here I was in this lonely lane with a donkey, night drawing upon us, and I could only imagine the familiar feel of my father's strong hand as I thought back to that other night excursion. But I could still sing. The first two lines of my mother's song came back to me.

Upward they vanish, through Gates of the West,
Upward to glory and onward to rest . . .

After this I was obliged to hum the tune only, for the words eluded me until I came to a line I was glad I had not forgotten.

Trust Him in Whom is no darkness at all.

No darkness at all . . .

As someone on a cliff ledge would rejoice in a rope flung down to them, I have found that in all life's circumstances one can rejoice in a single sentence expressing even a fragment of truth that can be grasped and believed. Such a sentence is the mental equivalent of a rope to a stranded person, and may be held on to by the simple process of slowly and continually repeating it in the silence of a mind in which it keeps all intruding thoughts and fears at bay. And so peace comes within one's own being – and where else indeed could it come, in the first instance? There can be no outward harmony if there is none within, for one is aware only of stress and turmoil.

So Darkie and I proceeded calmly on our way, and even

as I sang to myself I knew we would be in no great dilemma that night.

Soon I was remembering another period of singing in my life. It was not a happy time, but how we sang, my mother and I! Previously we had suffered two bereavements, my father and Victor having died within a year of each other, and because of my father's death the breaking up of our home in the country when we both went into service. And now it was 1914, and we were together in London, doing daily work and living in rooms in a block of buildings. In the evenings we would be doing our own domestic jobs, and often as I did the washing and my mother cooked the meal we would sing together.

I sang with my thoughts on Fred, away at the war. The songs of that war seemed to hold me closer to him. 'Somewhere in France, dear mother' and 'There's a long, long trail' were favourites, though they would often move me to tears. But we had a wide repertoire, ranging from hymns such as 'Growing together, wheat and tares' to light-hearted ditties from the music hall, my mother's speciality being 'Johnny used to grind the coffee mill'.

And then when Fred was home on leave, or his brother Bill, what times we used to have! The boys' father had bought a gramophone, a handsome affair with a large megaphone, and what a novelty it was in those days. As many of the neighbours in the buildings as could crowd into the small room would come to 'make a night of it' when we played our large assortment of records, and nobody seemed to mind the noise, which would perhaps have been more suited to a large hall. Not that the introduction of mechanical entertainment into our lives stopped us singing . . . when the records were put on we simply sang with them.

I have that old gramophone today, and many of the original records, and until recently would play it occasionally to hear the old songs. But in the last removal the sound box was damaged, so now I can no longer use it. I guessed it would be difficult to get a replacement. There it stands – a silent memento of so many musical evenings sixty years ago.

So deep was I in the past that I failed to realise at first that there was a car behind me. Certainly I had not expected it, and was momentarily harassed because the lane was too narrow for it to pass and I had no idea how soon my slow Darkie would reach a 'passing place', if indeed there was one. In our own lanes I am familiar with the exact position of these occasional widenings, scooped from adjoining field and re-topped by the hedge, thus making an oval haven which is the perfect retreat for Darkie and me. As I gaily wave the oncoming 'horseless carriage' on she settles for a rest and at the same time a snack of green from that inviting hedge. All these passing places are ours, for we know them intimately; the field gateways and slightly wider stretches of lane also. Out here, in unfamiliar territory, I could not even be sure of a passing place. For all I knew the fast moving car, or rather the car that by its very design was fast moving, would have to follow my slow donkey, a hare in low gear in step with a tortoise. And there was nothing I could do about it.

When there is nothing you can do about it the only thing to do is to keep going, striving to be as little harassed as possible. So I did, urging Darkie along as best I might, with at intervals the reward of two or three steps taken at a little trot before she eased back into her comfortable amble.

Thus it went on until I became aware of a teenage voice saying eagerly, 'May I take her bridle? I think if I draw her in a bit closer we shall be able to get by. We're quite small.'

I had a mischievous vision of a tiny white limousine driven by an elf, with a fairy in the back, though a pumpkin coach would perhaps have been nearer the mark. When I looked down I saw that contrary to my expectation she who had drawn level with the cart was anything but small – a tall, tanned young woman with a friendly, freckled face.

'We're quite small,' she repeated. 'Only a Mini. May I?'

'Oh yes,' I said. 'Please do.'

She had a kind word for Darkie and then, with admirable efficiency, manoeuvred donkey and cart the bare three or fours inches left to bring us to the edge of the lane.

'You're good with donkeys,' I said.

She laughed. 'I don't know about donkeys. I'm used to horses.'

Darkie and I waited with Darkie's usual patience for the Mini to inch its way by. White it certainly was, but its effect of filling the rest of the road with surely not an inch between itself and the cart destroyed any illusions about ethereal limousines.

The car was driven by an older woman, who smiled up at me as she passed. The girl waited by the donkey's head. When the car was safely by I asked her if she knew where I might get bed and breakfast and accommodation for the donkey. She looked at me in some astonishment.

'There's nothing along here,' she said. "It's just a lane leading out on to the main road.'

I carefully avoided asking how far to the main road – some things are better discovered for oneself – and knowing that when I reached there I could cross over into another lane with the hope of finding a farm, spoke as optimistically as I could about my prospects for the night.

She seemed a little dumbfounded as she climbed into the car, and then they were gone round the next bend and Darkie and I had the lane to ourselves again.

'Come on, Darkie,' I said – with a very *determined* jerk of the reins this time. A no-nonsense jerk, a positive declaration that this was no time for mere ambling, that I expected her to put her best foot forward.

'If you don't, Darkie,' I said with dreadful warning, 'you and I will be out *all night.*'

She evidently caught my mood for she did start off a little more briskly than usual, and to my satisfaction was soon moving at the steady plod with which, in a familiar lane, she always makes her homeward way. I was not very pleased when a couple of bends further along she was obliged to stop because a car was parked just ahead of us on the left hand side. Then I recognised the two people standing beside it and realised it was the Mini that had just passed us.

'Oh dear!' I thought. 'A breakdown!'

Donkey carts, I reflected, were far more dependable, but even while I was rejoicing in this, and from my high seat of satisfaction feeling a genuine sympathy with the car driver and her passenger, I realised that as far as Darkie and I were concerned we might just as well have broken down ourselves. For we were unable to get by.

Then, to my even greater surprise, the apparently stranded car driver expressed concern at what she evidently regarded as *my* predicament. I soon realised that these two were no mere passers-by on the road, but Good Samaritans.

They were mother and daughter, and having talked over my request for information about bed and breakfast now proposed that I should continue on my way to the main road, where it appeared there was a garage. The owner was a friend of theirs, and would most certainly house Darkie and her cart for the night, though he would not be able to take me in as well.

This seemed appropriate! She who was doing all the work on this tour had earned her bed. I could, if necessary, sleep in the cart. After all, I would not be the first to inhabit a stable for a night's lodging, I told myself.

They, however, had different ideas. When I got to the garage – I couldn't miss it, for it was right at the road junction – they would be waiting for me. As soon as the donkey was settled all I had to do was to hop in the car.

'You can come back with us,' said the little lady – she looked little beside her tall daughter. 'We've got plenty of room.'

'I'll say,' said the daughter. 'You can have a four-poster bed.'

'Now don't be silly, Jane . . .'

'And dine on woodcock tonight.'

Her mother was looking at Darkie. 'It'll take us about two minutes to get to the main road. How long will it take the donkey?'

I had no idea, and thinking they might be in a hurry I said that really it was all right and they must not wait for me. But they both said 'Nonsense' and before I could say any more had climbed back into the car and were driving off.

There was nothing for it but to try and get Darkie to 'hurry along quickly' as my old schoolmistress used to say. I reflected that my luck was certainly in, provided I could see Darkie comfortable, and I ceased to sing as I went along, being too intent upon my destination and at the same time wondering what kind of a bed I really *would* sleep in that night.

NEXT morning I would have liked to share with Darkie my pleasant musings over what I would tell them of my night's experiences when we reached home. I found this amusing, for I certainly didn't expect them to believe that I had slept in a four-poster bed. But I had.

It happened like this.

When Darkie finally ambled out on to the main road that evening, the Good Samaritans were still waiting. They were outside the garage they had spoken of, and with them was a man with a beard who looked at us as if he had never seen a donkey or a cart in his life. Well, perhaps he hadn't. Not both together, anyway.

Then he came to life and took hold of the bridle as we drew level with the group, and suddenly everyone was fussing round me. I was helped out, and we all seemed to be talking at once. Everyone moved very fast – except Darkie – and within ten minutes she had been unharnessed and bedded down in a barn behind the garage, where there was also plenty of room for the cart. After I had fed her there was barely time to say, 'See you in the morning' before I was whisked off and seated in the Mini, which itself took off at what seemed to me a tremendous speed. But then I am used to donkey pace.

All the way along we talked, chiefly about the donkey, but despite this and the speed of the car I had the impression that we were going quite a long way. There was no opportunity to ask questions, however, though I was intrigued by sentences they slipped in to each other about the time, whether they would be late with dinner, and if 'she' had definitely said there would be woodcock that night.

I was even more intrigued and not a little alarmed when the car turned into a wide drive between tall trees. For a moment I was back in a slower conveyance – not the donkey cart, but my father's horse-drawn oil van. Up just such a drive as this had he driven one day when I had been allowed a ride with him, and it had led, as my father said it would, past a mansion.

That imposing sight was imprinted upon my mind's eye, for he had told me to look at it, and I *had* looked, never having seen so large a house before. 'We shall be going past the front of the mansion,' he had said. 'So take a good look.'

We older people certainly inhabit more than one world. The present is ours; the past is ours too. We often have an inner world into which at times we retreat. Sometimes we may even inhabit the future for a brief space. No wonder some of us may at times appear to be in mental confusion. I am reminded of my own mother who used to give this impression a few months before she died. She, who had never at any time in her life had anything to do with cats, suddenly started 'seeing' them everywhere. In anguish she accused me of not feeding a poor starving one. Assuring her that there was no such cat only increased her distress. Six years later, on moving back into the country, I was suddenly inundated with stray cats, one of which was indeed starving. I remembered my mother then, and hoped she knew that I was feeding it.

So perhaps it is not to be wondered at that for a few moments I was out of that Mini on that dusky summer evening and seated on a high seat about the glossy backs of two powerful horses, the sun was shining bright with morning and banks of rhododendrons all in bloom rose up on either side of me. The owl's hoot from the trees which had greeted us when we turned into the drive had dissolved into a resounding chorale of many birds. An early summer morning somewhere around 1899 . . .

A few moments such as that can hold a memory complete in every detail, no matter how long the original happening took in the measurement of time. When the Mini slowed I had already completed my childhood drive and was past the mansion, and looking now at the large house in front of me it did not seem as imposing as the house of memory, which was perhaps just as well, though it was large enough to alarm me a little again, for grandeur is not in my line at all. It was homely accommodation I had been expecting. The

Good Samaritans had seemed perfectly homely people, so I was not prepared for this grey-stoned, many-windowed residence behind its green circle of trees.

I gave the classic exclamation. 'Oh dear!' I said.

'Don't worry,' said Jane kindly. 'We're slipping round the side here. Back door for us.'

'Back door?' I repeated, not yet able to grasp it. For if they did not qualify as ladies of the manor neither could I picture them as servants. Of course my ideas of servants belonged to the days of starched aprons and scrubbing brushes, and a parlourmaid I had known who washed her beautiful long hair only once a year, during her holiday, as she did not have sufficient time off in between in which to dry it. Servants who walked two miles to church in procession by order of their master while he and their mistress drove in the carriage . . . and here was Jane and her mother driving happily around the countryside in a car.

They ushered me into the large kitchen, explaining that they had dinner to prepare for the one lady at present in the household, but we would all have a cup of tea while they did it, and afterwards I could have supper with them.

'But won't Madam mind?' I asked them, going back to the old days with a bump – I who had been so meek and conscientious towards my 'Madams' when I was Jane's age.

Oh no, they assured me blithely, Madam wouldn't mind. They could entertain who they liked in their part of the house.

Their part of the house! And in addition to the kitchen I presently saw a comfortably furnished sitting-room with an electric fire and TV set, and three bedrooms and a bathroom on the floor above. In the sitting-room were various text books, and Jane told me she was going to take the Open University course.

And there was I back in the days when I was one of three maids sharing a bedroom, spending winter evenings in a corner of a candle-lit kitchen, my spare time devoted to making dolls' clothes at the request of my 'Madam' for church bazaars. Not that I minded. On looking back they seemed very cosy, happy evenings indeed, and the kitchen fairly buzzed with cheerful talk as we all sat busy as bees. I never had time, place or opportunity for the furthering of my education, but as the youngest of the servants I unconsciously absorbed plenty of knowledge as I sat with eager ears wide open to the talk. I was certainly well educated in the business of living.

'Stock,' said the house parlourmaid. 'That's what you want. Money hoarded up's no good. You want stock.'

The cook agreed with her. 'Stock's worth more than money.'

Their 'stock' was upstairs under their respective beds, safely stored in tin trunks. Lengths of material suitable for making up into frocks, skirts, blouses and aprons; a good supply of under-garments; innumerable pairs of thick stockings. And cook certainly needed plenty of 'stock' for her hat trimmings. After every third Sunday off would come the ribbon or flowers, and a completely different set of trimmings was carefully stitched in place, while the dolls' clothes remained for that evening in her workbox. And to all but the most discerning and those of us 'in the know' it would appear that cook had a new hat for church regularly once a month.

I said something of this in that other kitchen, not sure if I was in the past or the present, while Jane grimaced over the plucking of a woodcock. She had shown it to me before she began, and we had momentarily grieved together over the soft, limp bird with that distinctive plumage of various browns and black, that high forehead and long bill. Inconsistent as she had, for would we have so grieved over a chicken? But Jane confessed that the first time she had plucked one she did it with her eyes shut, and did not look until she had a kitchen floor deep in feathers and a corpse for the meat tin instead of that long-billed beauty of the woods.

I had supper with them – not woodcock, but ham and salad, which was certainly more to my liking. Jane had previously waited at table, and came down with the news that when I had finished supper 'Madam' would like to see me in the drawing-room. It was an extraordinary situation. I no longer seemed to be Daisy Baker, a mature pensioner, but Ellen Crockett, the ''tweenie' in her teens whose second Christian name had been deemed more suitable for 'in service' than the first, and who had received a summons to that other drawing-room where the elder of the Bishop's daughters for whom I worked at that time gave me weekly Scripture instruction.

When I followed Jane down the long corridor the illusion would have been complete had I felt a little more sprightly in the legs. But even as it was, when the door opened I half expected to hear that familiar voice saying kindly, 'Come along, Ellen. Let me hear if you have that psalm by heart today.'

For a moment I caught myself wondering which psalm I was supposed to have learned. And then the moment was gone, the past vanished as mist in morning sun, and there I was in the present – the whole of me. In the company of one as elderly as myself, yet revealing it so much less. She was tall in her high heeled satin slippers, elegant and evening-gowned.

I had no time to feel my conspicuous difference – sturdily shod, homely of hair style, simply dressed. She was smiling and holding out her hand, and speaking with a gentle courtesy. So there I was. Seated in a deep armchair and talking – of course – about Darkie again.

And such was the hospitality extended to me that night that I presently found myself going up not the steep back stairs but the front staircase that rose in a gracious curve, kind to the legs, taking in two landings on the way and gazed down upon by the portraits of the family's ancestors in the elaborate dress of their day. I was no longer Ellen the 'tweenie, nor was I quite myself. To tell the truth I was not sure I hadn't fallen asleep in the donkey cart, which was perhaps just as well as it saved me from being too conscious of the fact that I would have been more at home on the back stairs.

I had a bedroom overlooking a walled garden (as I discovered in the morning). And in the room was a four-poster bed. Jane assured me that it was by no means as large as the one in which Madam herself slept. Even so it was the largest and most elaborate bed I have ever slept in, and I was obliged to climb into it by means of a stool.

I was very grateful for a bed that night, but am not sure that I would care to sleep in such a stately one every night, despite the comfort of the deep mattress. Because of the box-like impression given by the four uprights and the overhead supports, I might in a half-sleep state have imagined I was riding high upon a hearse; but that night I hastily dismissed the association and concentrated upon more everyday matters.

That is what you must certainly do if you sleep for the first time in a four-poster! And do not draw the curtains that go with the bed. For there is no doubt that such beds have been slept in by a good many people, and your thoughts inevitably dwell upon them at first . . . the people who have slept and died in your bed. Curtains drawn, a mere fabric wall between you and the space of the room, are a finishing touch to a sense of the mysterious, setting you wondering if someone is drifting about on the other side of them. I hastily drew mine back again, and took advantage of the bedside lamp to read for a while.

But then again, I thought, what an ideal bed for the seating of the four saints! Out of childhood came the rhyme:

> Matthew, Mark, Luke and John,
> Guard the bed that I lie on.
> Four corners to my bed,
> Four angels round my head . . .

How easy to imagine two at the head and two at the foot, as I once saw in a drawing, when the 'corners' were as distinct as these!

And then it was back to earth, my final drifting to sleep in that strange bed being accomplished by mulling over thoughts of all the different beds I had slept in during the past seventy-odd years. Suddenly I recalled a word I had not heard or thought of for many a year. Was it my first bed, when I had slept upon a palliasse? Palliasse – what was it? Of course, a straw mattress. I imagine we shook it up, turned it over, and pounded it quite a bit for comfort, unlike today's spring mattresses. Now, at home, I had one of those, but out of the past came the feather beds, the lumpy flock mattresses, the iron bedsteads with the big brass knobs, the single beds, the double beds . . . and I think I fell asleep in my four-poster thinking I was really sleeping in my first double bed of all, back at home in East Grinstead, sharing it with my little brother Victor.

I dreamed, of course. Who would not, in a four-poster? Though they say we always dream, whether we remember or not in the morning. And in my pursuit of many beds I seemed, eventually, to be in Darkie's stable, and although I knew it was her stable it had all the strangeness that dream places so often have. Her familiar hay net was not there. Instead, plain enough to be recalled in the light of day, was a manger.

I REJOICED in my reunion with Darkie next morning, and when we had made our farewells to all the kind people who had helped us, I was glad – and I think she was too – to be on the road again. For there is nothing Darkie likes better than getting up in the morning.

At home she will rattle her door if we dare to be a little late opening it. She breathes loudly and half snorts as the top half is fixed back. Over the bottom half comes her nose on its breakfast quest. Ears now are half slanted, eyes on the roll, head tipped slightly back as she prepares to bellow her 'Good morning'. The greeting also conveys that it is high time her bowl had arrived.

A large square green bowl, well suited to a large nose, is put over, and she dives into her ration of flaked maize and carrots. When this is disposed of, she waits till she hears a footstep or catches a glimpse of a figure at the back door, then she will roar for the bottom half of the door to be opened. Darkie never wastes her voice on calling to people who aren't there. First she must see or hear someone, and then she will call. Perhaps she doesn't realise that her voice is more suited to a parade ground than a garden, harbouring the illusion that her tones have all the gentility of the ladies of Quality Street, for if she knew that she could be heard not only within the house but a mile down the road, she would surely not wait so patiently for someone to appear. Unless, of course, in this as in all things, she is simply being true to her nature, for patience is the essence of a donkey's character. She cannot help her loud voice; what we take for a demand could be a gentle reminder that please she is waiting, may she come? The whole performance is repeated again each night, when she is at the field gate ready to return to her stable. The patient wait; the uplifted voice at the first glimpse of someone coming. This morning and evening routine never varies.

On the road she does not as a rule 'speak' with her voice, only with her ears. I know her ear language pretty well now. And that morning after my rather exciting night I knew she was well content after *her* night's lodging as she set off with ears high, hoping, no doubt, that the verges and hedges of the lane I had chosen would be rich in snacks. For nothing makes a journey more pleasant than breaks en route.

I suppose she had had a dozen such breaks before we stopped for a legitimate one – to eat our lunch. At least, that I might eat *my* lunch. True I gave her carrots and biscuits, but hadn't she been eating her fill all the way along?

'Doubt if you want it, Darkie,' I said, but she did.

We had drawn in before a deep-set field gate, and the hedge there was such that the bank beneath it had certain comfortable indentations and small hollows that looked inviting to two parts of my anatomy I felt could do with a change of seat. So I sank into the soft grass and rested my back at the same time.

Through the gate I looked at a field of close cropped grass on which many sheep grazed, and thought about Matilda. I had called at two more farms that morning and had seen almost as many cats as sheep, including a high percentage of black and white ones. But not Matilda.

I ate fruit only, for I was not very hungry, and the warmth of the day was increasing. If it got too hot we could not travel for a couple of hours or so, for Darkie lags in heat, becoming slower than her usual amble, and I did not think it fair to her to insist upon her going along in the hot sun; for we, after all, were please-ourselves travellers, and so could put up in the village we were now approaching, instead of completing the day's mileage.

The flies troubled her too, buzzing persistently round her nose, and with my free hand I fanned her with a fern, resolving, when I had eaten my orange, to get out the paraffin rag I had brought and slightly smear it round her face, for these were horse flies and their nips are quite vicious digs into her flesh which can result in a sore place. The paraffin rag is not infallible, but it is a slight deterrent to these ardent biters.

I gazed at the sheep through the bars of the gate, and

some of the sheep gazed back at Darkie and me until we merged into the scenery, which made it unnecessary for them to investigate further or take alarm. Fat rumps made a solid wall of sheep as they turned to eat methodically in the other direction. I mused on the differences between this chubby, placid flock and the leggy, erratic goats; mused, too, with deeper insight into the Bible parable of the sheep and the goats and in my contemplation realised perhaps for the first time how very involved in everyday life Jesus must have been during those thirty years on earth.

He had observed the behaviour of real sheep and real goats; knew, too, the natures of each. I had not known this, but I knew it now. It made more sense of the story.

Take Tim, for instance. King Billy indeed! Dignity in every brown inch of him as he walks with grace to the field

each morning. But woe to anyone walking with him who is not familiar with the ways of billy goats (male goats, as I believe more realistic goat owners prefer to call them these days). He may pause, turn his head slightly, and scratch the middle of his back with the tip of one of those curved horns.

The movement and even the performance of its purpose is pure elegance; he loses not one whit of dignity. But having paused he may remain there a few moments, surveying the scenery. Quite maddening if it's before breakfast and the kettle is on the boil.

The unwary might urge him on. Woe, indeed! No longer remote and majestic, his head will again turn, front legs in a half leap with it, and if the broad part of the horns are aimed at you over you go – flat on your back. You don't feel anything, except the hard ground. It's worse to be knocked by a tip – a pain and a bruise for sure. No, it's never happened to me. I can handle my docile Darkie, but draw the line at billy goats. I have it on good authority, though, for it happened to Freda before she learned through experience how to handle him when he ceased to be a kid jumping in and out of an old armchair in the kitchen and being carried about and cuddled. He can, she says, be persuaded from a safe distance, responding to her voice if he is in the mood, and if not to remote control – a tug on his collar from the end of a rope.

Dignity to the winds too when he gambols in the field like any goatling, with skittish jumps and head bowings – the whole performance of goat gymnastics. And then the run at a butting post and the crash of horns on wood. Once he knocked the front out of a shed; we don't make that mistake now, but give him access.

And so I reflected on the waywardness of goat temperaments. Their desire at times to go in the opposite direction to that in which they are being led; to eat succulent things from the garden instead of grass in the field; to nibble at clothes on the line, eating the corners off towels and tea-cloths; to caress with loving nose one minute and butt the next.

For the purpose of a parable they are perfect. The sheep and the goats; the tractable and the perverse. But does that make them any the less loved? No, indeed – yet they must be banished when their behaviour is uncivilised. Certainly for all their waywardness we love ours as if they were all pet lambs, true love for an animal being, I suppose, unstinted attention to its welfare as well as a deep affection in the heart. We love them because we know them; for the way they answer to their names and respond to us; for their high intelligence, bright alertness and beautiful agility; even for the changing expressions in their eyes, and for their happiness as they busy themselves in being goats.

Darkie was pushing me with her nose. I had fallen into such a reverie about the sheep and the goats that I had forgotten her. The orange was eaten; I got up to attend to her. As I did so a bicycle bell rang.

'Hallo there!' cried a voice. 'How's the donkey?'

It was the girl with the cleaning fluid, who had shared the cart with me in the rain.

We exchanged pleasantries, and I explained how I came to be further from home than usual. Then I asked what luck she had had with her selling.

She was looking relaxed and happy, and said she had sold her first consignment of bottles and was now out with another, but laughingly denied that she was a good saleswoman.

'Pure luck,' she said, though admitted she was improving, and added, 'The things I could tell you!'

'Well, why not?' I said. 'It's hot, have a rest.'

So she fixed her bicycle and sat down. I put some more carrots in Darkie's bowl and joined her. This time I used the fern to fan myself.

'There was this guest house,' she said. 'The trouble was the chain had come off the bike, and my hands were looking a bit worse for wear. That woman really flattened me, though of course it was my own fault. She let me demonstrate the stuff and listened to everything, and then said, "Is that what it does to your hands?" No sale, but at least it taught me you've got to look as good as your stuff. So I suppose I should be grateful to her.'

I sympathised, and waited for the rest of the story.

'Such a lot of people say "No",' she sighed. 'I think you must get your "No" days when you're selling, for when you get one "No" it just seems to go on and on. I once went to a most inaccessible place – up a hill it was, and along a track, and then a whole lot of steps. And then when I knocked at the door an elderly woman opened it and she just snapped, "This isn't *my* house!" and slammed the door. Honestly, sometimes the world reminds me of *Alice In Wonderland*!'

She went on to tell me how she had sat in a chair guarded by two enormous dogs who showed their teeth if she moved an inch while their mistress went 'to ask my husband'. She had met a very old lady in a very new bungalow sitting in a cushioned chair on a deep pile carpet, the room quite spotless, and the old lady had smiled sweetly and said her house never needed cleaning, it just *stayed* clean.

'And then,' she said, 'I really did think I'd made a sale because there was this girl cleaning her windows, and right hard work she was making of it, rubbing away. She was interested at first, but directly she knew that my stuff made work easy she didn't want to know any more about it. She actually said she liked using elbow grease, and didn't feel she'd done the job properly otherwise.'

I laughed. 'That sounds more like my day than today.' And then I asked about her first success as a saleswoman.

She pulled a little face. 'I'll *never* forget that very first bottle I sold. I don't know about success – I nearly got done in!'

There was this man in the street, she said, cleaning his car. Now the Stuff she was selling cleaned everything, literally everything, including cars. Not just the bodywork. Windscreen, windows, upholstery, mats, even the engine. She made full use of this information, piling it on like cream on a cake.

She sprayed the windscreen and demonstrated how quickly it came up clean, without any effort at all. He was impressed.

'How much?' he asked.

'*What?*' he said, when she told him.

'That's terribly expensive,' he said, shaking his head.

She used all her wits and wiles to prove to him that it wasn't. How dilution was the secret . . . how long a bottle of the Stuff Itself would last him. He held a bottle and fingered it with what she could see was the longing of ownership upon him. She pressed her points home . . . the economy in the long run . . . the easy cleaning . . . the swift and perfect result . . .

'All right, I'll have one,' he said.

But he didn't have the money on him. It appeared he lived up a little back alley between the cottages, and if she called at No. 3 on her way back he'd be there to pay her.

She knocked at No. 3 after a tiring afternoon and no more sales. There was a glow of comfort inside her, however, because at that house no further effort was required and all she had to do was to collect the money.

It was not her obliging customer who opened the door,

however. A woman stood there – quite a small woman, but every inch of her sparking with anger.

'So it was you who caught him!' she began accusingly, and then launched on a long tirade about how easily unwary men are parted from their money. There was she, eking and paring with the housekeeping, and there was he throwing pound notes away – or rather, there was the girl wheedling them out of him.

Inside a plaintive voice remonstrated, calling persistently to the woman, but not until she had had her say did she take any notice, and then she shut the door – hard.

The girl stared at the door in disbelief. She had either got to have her money or the bottle back, and she was not sure what to do. It would have taken courage to knock at that door again. Fortunately her dilemma was solved when it slowly opened. She watched in fascination as a hand was extended through the aperture, offering her the money while a voice whispered, 'Here, take it. And thanks very much. Sorry about all that.'

We laughed together. Then she said, 'Well, I must be off,' and springing up jumped on her bicycle and was away, calling 'Nice to see you,' over her shoulder.

'Youth!' I sighed to Darkie, and tried to remember the last time I had moved so nimbly. But perhaps there had not been a last time . . . imperceptibly come the signs of age, and as summer merges into autumn so do we ourselves merge into the different stages of our lives. Which is just as well, I reflected, or we would be strangers to ourselves instead of keeping on a familiar footing. It is only in looking back that we come to realise how we have changed from the child, the youngster, the young and middle-aged adult, and then comes the astonished thought, 'Was that really *me*? Was I really like that?' And you think you are looking back at another person who has no relation to yourself at all.

How nice, though, to settle comfortably into each stage as it comes, enjoying the best of it, which I really think I have done, even though I now believe I have reached the most satisfying stage of all. At least, for me. Who wants to engage in battle with inexorable minutes, using every device and subterfuge to snatch a victory from the ever-active hands of time once they have discovered the great secret? The secret that time is a friend.

I in my donkey cart have made friends with time, accepting and forgetting the passage of the days that fly so close together, like flocks of birds, in successive formations of seven. Now that there is no longer any need to attempt to keep up with the gathering momentum of the weeks that hustle so soon into a year I tend to inhabit more and more the timeless regions of dream and memory. That there are such regions surely renders time of little real account, except to make sense of our earth life as it takes us from one stage of growth to the next and through the myriad experiences we seem to need – to make us, perhaps, into more enlightened beings?

How often in the past, in my desire to retain the moment, or even to escape the moment, have I overlooked the fact that life is quite literally a journey. As distinct and real a journey as if we deliberately set out somewhere on foot or entered a car or train or even a donkey cart. On journeys the scenery changes, people stop at different places and part company. Nor can you stay to look at the view too long. I have found that once the fact that life is a journey is accepted, once I have actually realised I am adventuring through this world to go one day beyond it, the burdens that tend to accumulate on the way become lighter.

I knew nothing of the friendliness of time when I walked the streets of London at night with my eyes raised high above the buildings asking, 'Why? Why did it have to happen? Why?' That frail human cry that has echoed throughout the ages. Yet when Freda was a tiny child I could tell her happy bedtime stories about her Uncle Fred, the boy soldier she had never seen, and marvelling say those old, true words, 'Time is a wonderful healer.'

It took me much longer to discover that those moments of joy, of intense pleasure, of beauty perhaps, or perception down to the kernel in the shell, not only cannot be held stationary that we may live in them for ever, but would indeed lose their identity if we did so. After all, the whole purpose of a journey is to keep going until one gets there, and I, looking towards the horizon of life in this world with my shortening earth sight, felt all the thrill of one upon whom heaven's sight is bestowed. I fell to wondering if the journey ever does in fact have a precise and permanent 'end' in any particular 'place' or 'time' or always respites, like that one at the roadside, before new experiences make new horizons.

The girl on the bicycle had gone out of sight. It was very hot. While she knocked at unresponsive cottage doors I drowsed over my thoughts without a conscience to prod me into doing something else. Such is one privilege of age.

And I still had tomorrow.

I SPENT that night in a room at a village pub, which, being a wayfarer, I described to myself as an inn. They no longer kept accommodation for wayfarers like myself, of course (with horses or donkeys), but Darkie was comfortably bedded down in an outhouse.

As we set out next morning I wondered what this day would bring forth. So far each day had been interesting. I had not found it tiring; neither had Darkie. Our casual pace and resting places had taken good care of that. We had not got wet, for there had been no rain. The cart was rolling gently along in good working order. Thinking of all this I was well content. But there was still the best part of four days to go – looking ahead it might have been four years! So unable was I to assess time upon this seemingly timeless journey when the only routine was that of moving slowly along, stopping at certain points, and starting off again.

'Supposing you get a puncture?' Freda's voice sounded in the ear of my memory. 'Supposing it rains? Supposing you don't feel well or Darkie can't keep it up?'

With four days still to go I was not going to suppose any such things. On the contrary, I was looking forward to fresh delights. Here was I, out upon the highway with my donkey, going places! 'Oh what a beautiful morning, oh what a beautiful day!' Yes, I really did have a beautiful feeling. Everything *was* 'going my way'. I told myself this most decisively in answer to that voice in my memory and the thought of the four unknown days ahead. For there does come a point on a journey when a traveller can have forebodings, or strange imaginings, and I already knew the golden rule to overcome these. And that is to discipline one's thoughts.

I once lived next door to a young couple with their first

baby. The child was about three weeks old, and she was crying, and through their open window to mine came the sound, followed – to my amusement – by the young father's voice speaking in tones of good-tempered but very firm advice. 'Don't let her master you Hilda!'

Such strange things at unexpected moments does memory come up with, and the trivial incident flashed back into my mind at that moment, apparently having no bearing whatsoever upon what I had been thinking about. Yet I knew, on deeper consideration, that it had. Our 'inside' mind behind our conscious thoughts is wiser than we are, and the key word was 'master'. There was the link that had produced the memory. The disciplining of thoughts, even as one would discipline a child.

To master oneself is perhaps more difficult than to master another person. Yet like most things it is easy enough when you know how, and all a matter of practice. I knew this. It is not so very long ago that I learned the basic principle – I am the one thinking the thoughts; they are not thinking me! Therefore I am in control of them. If they become wayward I simply change them. For if we are free anywhere it is within our own minds. We can think what we like.

And so that morning I deliberately changed thoughts of punctures, rain, of not feeling well during the coming days, and delighted myself in thinking of the new and unexplored territory ahead, the ever changing views of sky and landscape that would open up, the friendly greetings I would exchange with people I had never seen before, the quiet rests and little meals, and the comfortable bed that somewhere awaited me at the end of the day. And perhaps – who knew? – this might be the day when I would find Matilda.

As sure as you think of nice things, sooner or later the harmony of your thought will attract them to you. Just as we may have more to do than we realise with the unpleasant things that happen to us. But on that morning I did not anticipate quite such a happy time as I had that afternoon.

But to begin at the beginning. It really began with Darkie's hat.

It grew very warm again about midday, and soon the flies began their perpetual dance around Darkie's nose. I applied the paraffin rag without any noticeable effect. Not much use saying, 'Oh, poor Darkie,' as she continually ducked and shook her head, but what could I do? I decided we would call a halt in the next shady place and have an early lunch.

Before we got to it, however, we passed a cottage. Leaning over the gate was an old man. As I said 'Good morning,' to him Darkie decided to stop.

'Fine looking donkey you got there,' he said. 'Come far?'

I felt as seasoned a traveller as if we had crossed half a continent. The mileage didn't matter. We measured it, she and I, by every unfamiliar inch of every unknown lane, by every new sky-line, by every face we had not seen before, and by every breath of air we took.

When I told him about the journey he was not impressed. 'Go on, you should be getting along twice as quick as that!'

'But I didn't want to be quick!' I protested.

'What you want,' he said, 'is a switch. Like this.'

He plucked a thin hazel branch from the hedge and before I could stop him had applied it lightly to Darkie's hind quarters. She leapt forward a couple of feet, nearly unseating me, then stopped and shook her ears. I thought the backward roll of her eyes was reproachful, and wanted to say, 'It wasn't me, Darkie!'

'There y'are,' said the old man. 'Here, take it, missus. Just you give her a tap with it on her backside when she dawdles. You'll get there twice as fast.'

I couldn't help smiling.

'It may be the thing to do,' I said, 'but I'm in no hurry. I like her to go her own pace. We get there just the same.'

He could see no sense in my argument, and did not mince his words in saying so. A donkey was transport, and that was that. And transport should move. As fast as its horse power or donkey power could propel it. He recalled the days when he rode a donkey bareback between his home and the town, and though he was prepared to admit it took half a day he reckoned *his* donkey *moved*. Certainly faster than mine.

'Them flies is a pest,' he said. 'Ever tried her with a hat?'

I looked at him in astonishment. 'A hat?'

'Wait a minute,' he said.

He turned, then half-way down the garden path looked back. 'Got a minute, have you?'

'I always have plenty of minutes,' I assured him.

'Come on in then,' he said. 'Tie her to the gate-post. Don't matter about the hedge. Needs cutting.'

Darkie was already nosing at the mixed hedge of hazel and hawthorn, and as we were in shade from trees, which I had been seeking, I thought his invitation a good idea. I climbed out of the cart, tied Darkie, and stepped inside the gate.

The old man had disappeared into dim regions beyond a small porch darkened and enclosed by overhanging creepers.

'Take a seat,' his voice came back to me.

I could see nothing to sit on but a tree stump in the middle of the small lawn, and I didn't suppose he meant that. Then I noticed the porch had a plank seat at one side of it, so I went in and sat down, alongside a geranium. The pleasant smell of the plant mingled with the cool air, which was refreshing on coming in from the sun.

There were various sounds within, and presently the old man emerged.

'What she wants is an old straw hat,' he said. 'I've got one somewhere about. But you come on in – the wife'd have summat to say, you stuck out there.'

'It's all right – ' I began, but he waved the words aside and pulled the door wider.

'I got a pot o' tea on the go,' he said. 'Or would you like some scrumpy?'

Hastily I settled for the tea.

I decided to enjoy this unexpected hospitality, and sitting down in a chair with wooden arms beside a windowsill green and flowery with many plants generously overflowing their pots, accepted the tea he proffered me in a good old-fashioned breakfast cup.

He did not keep me company; he was hunting about in other rooms, and presently emerged with an ancient straw hat the colour of a well baked biscuit.

'Here 'tis,' he said, thrusting it at me.

'But – how can she wear this?' I asked, bewildered.

'What?' he chuckled. 'A'nt you never seen a donkey in a hat?'

'Never!' I said.

'You'll see,' he said. 'But drink your tea first in peace.'

I drank my tea in peace, and while I did so ventured to ask if by any chance he had seen a black and white cat around.

'No cats here,' he said. 'Nor dogs neither. Company they

may be, but who's to feed 'em when there's nobody here? They wasps make a bit o' company in the summer, and a mouse or two in the winter.'

'Wasps?' I said. I thought he must mean bees, and looked around as I spoke for I had been aware for some time of a rhythmic humming. He pointed to the dresser.

'Wasps,' he said.

On the dresser stood a saucer of sugar. At least, a saucer with a white frill of sugar. The centre was a solid mass of little yellow and black bodies, all on the wriggle. Above the saucer more wasps were circling, and this accounted for the humming sounds I had heard.

'Keeps 'em happy,' he said. 'Stops 'em making holes in the sugar bags.'

'You don't go for the new-fangled way then,' I said.

'What, sprays?' he said. 'No, I don't. Them's all right so long as they're behaving themselves, and I don't grudge 'em a bit o' sugar. As much right to live as I.'

'Yes, I agree with you,' I said.

He chuckled, and lowered his voice. 'The wife don't, though.'

'Well,' I said, 'I suppose it *is* her kitchen. But it looks as if she's broad-minded about it.'

'Broad-minded?' he said. 'Her? Never broad-minded in her life. She knows the way 'tis, though. They're a bit o' company, and 'tis interesting studying 'em.'

'Yes,' I said, rather fascinated now by this wasp saucer. I noticed how the wasps all preferred to mill together in one big heap among the trodden sugar rather than seek to separate into the virgin whiteness round the rim. Each small body was vibrating with action in complete harmony.

He picked up a large pair of scissors and proceeded to cut two holes in the crown of the straw hat.

'See?' he said. 'Them's for her ears.'

'Oh,' I said doubtfully. I didn't think Darkie would be very keen. If there is one thing she dislikes it is her ears touched. I couldn't quite see her submitting willingly to having them stuck through the holes in a hat.

'There y'are,' he said. 'That'll keep a bit o' sun off and diddle the flies a bit.'

We went outside to introduce Darkie to The Hat.

Darkie stretched out her nose towards the object in case

it should contain eatables. She drew her head up when she
found it did not, but he had a way with donkeys and in no
time her ears were through those holes and the hat with its
wide brim was perched upon her head as firmly as if secured

with hat pins. I couldn't help laughing at the change in her
appearance. She endeavoured to answer me with her questioning ears, but the hat now restricted their up and down
movements. As she likes talking with her ears I decided that
the disadvantage of this restriction might outweigh any
advantages of The Hat, but obviously a fair trial was called
for, so when I was settled in the cart I thanked the old man
sincerely for it, and also for the tea, and said I was sorry to
have missed seeing his wife.

He gave a strange little smile.

'Bless us,' he said, 'you've missed her by a twelvemonth.
I don't never think of it, but must be nigh a twelvemonth
since she's been down churchyard.'

Before I could say anything he swished at Darkie with
the hazel twig, thrust it into my hand as she stepped smartly
forward, and called after us, 'Mind how you go, missus!'

I sat there rather dazed with the hazel in my hand, only
vaguely aware that Darkie was keeping up her pace. He had
spoken so naturally of his wife, as if she was somewhere close
at hand, and then I realised how right he was, and how
courageous. A life-time of companionship cannot be sun-

dered by death; in thinking and speaking of her as he did he preserved what the years had built up, and so was helped in completing the daily journey of the days alone.

While I was thinking and dreaming Darkie settled into her comfortable amble again. She seemed to have accepted The Hat, so I left it, and there it stayed for the rest of the morning, while we rested for our lunch and when we set off again in the afternoon. The flies were certainly less troublesome.

It was later that afternoon, as we went dreaming along, that the unexpected happiness began. We rounded a bend in the lane and coming towards us in the distance was a group of small children. Their shrill, excited voices reached me before I could distinguish them properly, and then as we drew nearer I saw there were five of them, three little girls and two boys. And all five were staggering along overloaded with laughter.

Darkie and I stopped by mutual consent as they came up to us, surrounding her. The questions flew to my ears like little piping birds.

'Why is your donkey wearing a hat?'

'Does he belong to a circus?'

'Is it a he or a she?'

'Where are you going?'

'Where have you come from?'

I made up a story for them. 'We've come a long way, and we've got a long way to go. We're searching for a little cat with a black head and face and back, and a white chest, white whiskers and four white paws. Her name's Matilda, and the donkey's name is Darkie. She's wearing a hat to keep the sun out of her eyes, and soon she will be tired and want to go to bed until tomorrow. Do you know where we could stay for the night?'

They were fascinated, and another chorus chirped up.

'You can stay at my house!'

'I'll ask my mum – she takes people.'

'Oh, please come and stay with me!'

Hating to dampen their enthusiasm, I said, 'But I don't suppose any of you have got anywhere that the donkey can sleep, have you?'

To which I received the instant reply from a little ginger-haired chap, 'She can sleep in my bedroom!'

I explained to them that what I really wanted was a farm-house.

'Her uncle's got a farm,' they said, looking at the smallest child, a little girl of about three.

'My uncle's got a farm,' she echoed.

'Then perhaps I can go there,' I said. 'Can you tell me the way?'

They all spoke at once, and then it seemed that they were going that way themselves, and that it was not very far down a winding lane to the right of us.

'Would you like to ride with me?' I asked the smallest girl.

That did it. I quickly had three of them in the cart. The other two led Darkie, one each side of her. But not for long. One of the little girls soon had the bright idea of picking flowers as we went along and making a garland for Darkie's hat. The other girls and one of the boys quickly joined her, and soon The Hat was wreathed in honeysuckle that trailed over her mane, her harness was stuck with sprigs of cow parsley and red campion, and foxgloves stood out of the holes in The Hat, topping her ears.

They were overjoyed with the results of their labours, and we were a merry party as we wound our way slowly round the bends in the lane. I don't know what Darkie thought about it all, but she went along as placidly as ever.

We stopped to let a car pass. The car stopped too, and several people got out. They were foreigners, and I couldn't understand a word they were saying, but saw they were smiling broadly as they gesticulated. Then one of them came forward and said politely, 'We take a picture? English carnival?'

'No, it's just me and my donkey,' I told him. 'But you can take a picture if you like.'

They all took pictures, and the children were delighted. Then the young man pressed something into my hand before I could stop him, murmuring 'For the carnival', and they were gone.

I saw he had given me a fifty pence piece, and looking at the children thought, 'Oh well, five into fifty goes ten,' so taking out my purse I changed it into ten pence coins and distributed the largesse. They were certainly having an afternoon to remember – and so was I!

When we reached the farm I was greeted by a pleasant

middle-aged woman who was only too pleased to provide beds for Darkie and me. I began to think we might settle a little early that evening, after all the excitement, but it seemed the day was not yet over.

Looking at the children milling round the cart, she said wistfully, 'What a pity Lindy isn't here. Poor little thing. She missed the fête Saturday, and she was so disappointed.'

I asked about Lindy and learned that she had been ill and was still confined to the house, where she had been for some time. The children were pulling at the reins and crying, 'Let's go to Lindy's! Let's take the donkey to see Lindy!'

The three-year-old, who was piping the loudest, was hushed by her aunt. I asked how far it was to Lindy's, and was told about ten minutes' walk, but not to think of taking the trouble to go.

I was tempted to say that we would go and see Lindy in the morning, but realised that Darkie and her floral hat and the general air of carnival the foreign visitor had felt generating around us belonged to today and not to tomorrow. In the morning the children would be dispersed, The Hat removed, the flowers withered.

'Oh, we must go to Lindy's!' I said. 'Would you like to go to Lindy's, Darkie?' I jerked the reins at the same time, and Darkie took a step forward. The children cheered.

'Come on,' I called. 'Let's go to Lindy's!'

THE lane to Lindy's seemed very long. Or perhaps it was that Darkie was very slow. I am not usually aware of time, but that evening I felt the estimated ten minutes represented a brisk walker's pace rather than an ambling donkey's.

Not that the journey was not enjoyable. I found the children's chatter amusing, and as for them *they* would have been content to travel with Darkie for twice as long.

They pointed out to me the secrets of the lane. Where the hazel nuts grew, and the biggest blackberries; the little paths trodden down the bank by pheasants from the woods, a nest where a robin had laid eggs in the spring, and a 'camp' they had made in the ditch with bracken.

A boy and a girl ran on ahead. We were nearly to Lindy's. Arriving at a cottage, its window abutting on the lane, we saw the pale face of little Lindy pressed to the glass, all beaming smiles. As we drew alongside Darkie turned her inquisitive nose towards the window, which the little girl immediately pushed up. She was then able to stroke Darkie's nose, and I hastily produced some carrots so that she could feed her too. Once again The Hat went down well. A donkey alone would have been a tonic to a child confined to the house, but a donkey in a *hat* . . . !

At last Darkie was bedded down for the night, and I was looking out at the stars from the window of a bedroom in the farmhouse. An enchanting window set deep in the wall, its wide sill only just above the level of the floor. I might have sat there and star-gazed for a while, but I was tired, and knew I would sleep well.

I did; and woke to find the sun well risen. My substantial breakfast eaten, I felt well set up till nightfall, and when Darkie had had her breakfast of maize and carrots both of us were ready for the road.

There was no one to see us off; as I had foreseen the night before the children were elsewhere, the flowers had faded, The Hat no longer adorned Darkie's head, but was stowed away in the back of the cart for possible future use – as entertainment value it seemed to me, rather than anything else! I was glad we had gone to see little Lindy the evening before when the excitement had been at its height.

I went back to the farm to tell them I was just off, returning to Darkie and the cart a few minutes later feeling

like a traveller of Biblical days who had received a blessing, so warm were the good wishes for the successful completion of my journey.

'Good girl, Darkie! On we go!' And she was off, slow footed but sure.

As we went down the lane I became aware of something odd. There was a sound I could not quite place. It disturbed me for a few yards, and then I halted Darkie and listened intently. For a moment, nothing. Then a very distinct scratching.

It seemed to be coming from the back of the cart, so I turned round in my seat and investigated. There was nothing to be seen at a glance, but on moving my raincoat I saw there was a box underneath it which certainly didn't belong to me. I drew it nearer; it seemed heavy. For a moment I thought perhaps it was not scratching I had heard, but ticking! Surely not a bomb!

Instead of an explosion there came a faint cry. A piece of paper attached to the lid of the box provided the explanation. Scrawled on it in a childish hand were the words, 'Here is a blak and wite kat for you. Her name is Whisky. Luv, Gordon.'

Marvelling at the ways of children, I lifted the lid slightly. Perhaps by some miracle it *was* Matilda, found and renamed. But within the box was a white head with a black patch, and a body also patched black and white. Not Matilda's serene black face and white whiskers, and her white shirt front looking out at me. I stroked the head and hastily replaced the lid of the box, wondering which of the little boys had made me this gift. His own beloved pet parted with, a straying cat rounded up? I could not tell, but after some thought wrote him a little note on the back of his own.

'Dear Gordon, Thank you for giving me Whisky. I am sorry I cannot keep her. It is Matilda I'm looking for. When I find her she would not like me to take Whisky home too, so I know you won't mind if I give Whisky back to you. It was very kind of you to give her to me. Love from Darkie and me.'

I now had the problem of returning the cat to the farm. At that part of the narrow lane I could not turn the cart round. Nor could I carry the heavy box with the cat in it, even if I decided to leave Darkie there waiting, which I did not care to do. And I couldn't carry the cat without the box in case it jumped out of my arms and ran away. If it did it would obviously return home, but this was not exactly the way to return a little boy's gift.

My dilemma was solved when two girls came along the lane.

'Do you happen to know a little boy called Gordon?' I

asked, and learned that Gordon lived in the village in the direction I was going. So I continued on my way, cat and all, and hoped it would not be too long before I could return poor imprisoned Whisky to her everyday life. Even so I resisted the idea of applying a hazel twig to Darkie's rear, and we proceeded at our usual moderate pace.

It was early in the day for reverie, yet as we went along I fell into my customary musing. I was tantalised by the words I had just said, 'A little boy called Gordon', and couldn't think why. Then back across the years came my mother's voice, singing. And the title of the song came vividly back to me – 'A little boy called Taps'.

A sentimental, tear-filled song, as so many of them were at that time. Taps was not so very little, except to the 'old eyes' of his mother, for he was old enough to answer the bugle call to some war or other. I wondered if it could have been the Boer War – and there I was, back in the old days again.

Childhood days of serenity and peace, of a small, snug world – or were they? I had been so safely enclosed it had not seemed then that there was any bad thing in the world, or that my private world or the bigger world within which we lived would ever change. I did not know then that change is an essential part of life, nor did I even realise that I was changing all the time myself, from babyhood to child-hood, to adolescence, to adult. I was me! That's all there was to it at every stage. And I thought the world was a good place, perhaps because the media as we know it today did not exist to report to us the terrible doings of those who lose the way on their journey and wander in the back streets of existence instead of exploring the signposted road ahead. No television; no radio. In our house not even a newspaper. I cannot remember seeing a newspaper as a child.

People will lose their way in every generation, and the emphasis today is all upon the lost ones. We know so little of the undetected good that manifests in lives as ordinary and unreported as our own, just as in my childhood much less was known about the bad. Quiet country days were mine in a world that seemed to have been created out of the peace of the stars and the hills. Peace and simplicity harmonised in our daily lives. Horses' hooves on the roads, and leisurely steam trains puffing their plumes of white smoke into our otherwise unpolluted air. A candle in the bedroom, and a brick warmed in the oven and wrapped in red flannel comforting a cold bed on a wintry night. Watercress growing by the stream, free for everybody's tea. And the timeless hours and days, weeks, months and years, and we in the safe centre of this changeless ocean, borne upon its gentle waves without realising we were being wafted to a shore, on to a road as different as our white dusty ones were to the tarmac of today.

At what point did we 'land'? Individual family tragedies there may have been, but the real change came with the explosion of our world in 1914. Yet, I reflected, enjoying my different kind of peace with Darkie, out of great sorrow is the spirit born. And outward change can stabilise the inward self and so bring a new changelessness. For let the world change how it will, when we become thoroughly acquainted with ourselves and the true nature of all that is, we live upon an unshakable foundation no matter what happens in the outer world.

And so I resurrect the peace of my childhood in the deep places of my heart. Then it was a peace dependent upon everything remaining the same for ever, upon my own interpreting emotions. Now emotions drift away like falling autumn leaves, and I am what I am – as rooted as the tree from which the leaves fall.

As usual I came out of my reverie because Darkie had stopped. And not to eat. Just to stand motionless, waiting. Dreaming like me, perhaps? She is a great one for companionable awareness of what I am engaged upon in the cart behind her. Maybe she misses the few words I speak to her from time to time, and not hearing my voice concludes that I am concentrating upon something other than her. And so she stops. Taking advantage? Well, maybe. But who am I to deny a donkey her moments of reverie when I enjoy so many of my own?

However, as the old man at the cottage had pointed out to me, she is my transport and transport must move. So on we went towards the village.

I left Gordon's cat and my little note to him with his mother, and made my way to the next farm I intended calling at. Again many cats, but not Matilda. There was a pleasant resting place not far from here. A herd of cows had

110

just left a field for milking, and the field gate still stood invitingly open. In went Darkie and I.

She browsed and dreamed in the sun while I, comfortably seated upon a wrap from the cart, rested my back against the bank and looked at the view. Only this time there wasn't one – at least, not the usual pattern of field upon hilly field, of woods, farmhouses, and sometimes the sea: 'usual' yet always with a variation, a delightful individuality of landscape presenting the same countryside in fresh aspect. But in this field the view was of the one field itself, the one field and the sky. It was not a steep field, but once in it the gentle slope appeared to meet the sky-line.

I was sitting in the field, but it seemed as if I was not far from the sky, had only to walk up the field, in fact, to enter a new dimension. Skyscape instead of landscape: undulating downs of pale blue leading me over vast space to mountain ranges of white peaked cloud, perhaps, or golden lakes of sunset. I smiled, for surely donkey pace would not do for those regions. Wings, rather, or a light, aerial body floating on air.

And then I realised. My mind was that light body – my free, exploring mind, which no physical body could confine. In my mind I could go anywhere, do anything, even while I sat upon the hard ground. And the more my mind roved the less conscious would I be of the hardness of the ground that kept my feet so solidly upon it.

It was there, where the sky seemed to touch the earth, that like a child I re-learned an old truth that came new to me; the very *nearness* of heaven. A heaven not measured by height or depth, but on the very borders of our awareness. Surely, I thought, it is only awareness we need to pass the threshold.

And beyond? As my whole vision filled with field merging into sky I knew that it was a matter of feeling rather than seeing. First that tremendous awareness of *life – life itself*. Not our active life in the world, the adventure of it all, the immense sorrows and sufferings, but the creative force animating us and all creatures, making the grass flourish, the tides ebb and flow, fashioning a mountain or a stone. Life *itself*. The real thing, the *living* life, the vibrant, vibrating, vital life force in everything. And then to feel that very life force flowing within one's own being – to feel, to know instead of taking every breath, every movement simply for granted in the plain routine of day succeeding day. To have that moment out of time, when time is no more than a passing dream, that moment of feeling and knowing ... and in that awareness of life within oneself as a reality rather than a mechanism to reach even further into the unknown, that – who knows? – at some stage before birth may even have been the known, and to feel part of a whole. No longer a solitary spirit within one of many separate bodies, but inwardly linked to that same life force in all.

Yes, I reflected that day in the field, this was the very gate of heaven. But only the gate. To pass further one must go further. Surely it takes the whole of our very being to complete the transition from earth to heaven. And more even than this. I seemed to feel the earth that day held within the embrace of the encircling sky; and within the sky, the air, was the life force too, and the universe itself held in this great power. And it was a power of immense tenderness and love, for this paternal life spirit, creating and reproducing in so many forms throughout the universe, surely has an element of the maternal also. This, for me, is the way through the gates, just beyond the very threshold of heaven. All questioning is put aside, mere clothing that conceals the spirit, and my naked spirit basks in a realisation of the divine love that now flows with such comfort into me, as sun bathers put aside their clothes and bask in the warmth of the sun. For to feel is to know, and to know with the heart is to puzzle no longer over the intellectual questionings of the brain.

No, it is not the ostrich burying its poor deluded head into the apparent safety of the sand. For in such a moment of contemplation of heaven your feet, after all, remain upon the earth, and when you return from the journey your heart and mind have taken it is with greater strength and sometimes with deeper understanding. I do not close my eyes to the evil in the world, to the troubled times, but I feel I know now beyond self-contradiction that whatever is wrong within this world, even within our own individual selves and lives, or even in the world of nature, is never, never what the divine love-power that created us all intended. We have been given our world and the precious gift of free will and when things are wrong the responsibility is ours, and ours also the responsibility for putting it right.

In putting things right in my own life I know that the surest way of doing so is to ask and *expect to receive in answer* help from the highest source of all help, all love, all power. Whatever is written anywhere, in any book, even the Bible with its apparent contradictions and veiled teachings, it is within our own hearts and all that our hearts can contact that the truth is found. We search and find; we find and keep, for when we know for ourselves nothing and no one can take that knowing away. And so I gently merged into my knowing that afternoon where the earth merged gently into sky.

How lumbering words seem . . . as pedestrian as my plodding donkey. They put flesh upon my bodiless thoughts, but how little they convey. A whisper in a secret place, a shout upon a rooftop – it is all nothing compared with a moment of truth in one's own heart. How near some are to such experiences . . . how far others have to go.

I do not know how long I stayed in the field. On such mental excursions as mine any amount of time may pass, or I can be there and back in a moment, marvelling that time set me no limits in that other dimension.

Blue sky, green earth, brown donkey – they were all there again. And the ground as solid as ever. I got up in a hurry. Darkie and I would have to be on our way before the cows returned.

THAT day I had news from home.

I felt like a traveller in a far country, receiving unexpected mail and suddenly homesick. Only mine wasn't mail. My telephone call to the farm chanced to coincide with Freda's arrival there, as, still inhabiting somewhat timeless regions, I was later than usual in making the daily call.

It seemed strange hearing her voice, as if weeks had passed instead of days. She bubbled with questions.

'Are you really all right? Is Darkie all right? What have you been doing? Did you have any difficulty putting up at nights, and are you having enough to eat? You're not over-doing it? Oh – and any news of Matilda?'

Regretfully I told her there was no news of Matilda. But I had not given up hope. There was still time.

'You're sticking it out then?' she said.

'Sticking it out!' I said indignantly. 'I'm enjoying myself!'

Impossible to describe all my doings into the impersonal mouthpiece of a telephone. I closed my eyes to see her face, but it didn't work, so I said she would have to wait for my news until I returned home – and meantime was there any news her end?

It seemed most unlikely that there would be, for life at home proceeds uneventfully as a rule. But there might have been something interesting in the post.

'News!' said Freda. 'Things haven't stopped happening since you left. We've had the Council inspection for the bathroom grant, and I think it'll be all right. They seemed to think the house has got a life of fifteen years, anyway! Susy had to have a little operation to remove a tumour, and we nearly lost King Billy.'

My head whirled. All my little adventures of the past few days whirled away at the same time as if they had never been.

114

'Susy?' I managed to say. 'Is she all right? And how on earth could you lose Tim?'

How *did* one lose a billy goat?

I was assured that Susy was fine and didn't even know what had happened to her. Back on the log pile, ratting. As for Tim – well, he hadn't been really lost, though he might have been.

'I had the three goats in the lane,' said Freda. 'I was bringing them up from the bottom gate. Tim stopped to eat, but Snow and Frisky went on up. I'd forgotten to lock the kitchen door, and you know what they are – they'd have been in raiding the cupboard, so I went with them, thinking Tim would make his way after us. While I was settling them I heard a car go along the bottom, but it didn't bother me because I thought Tim was coming up. Then I went back for him, but he wasn't in the lane, so I realised he must have turned the other way, into the road.'

'The car hit him?' I exclaimed.

'No! I ran all the way down, but when I got there he wasn't there. He just wasn't anywhere to be seen. Vanished!'

'Vanished?' I said, feeling in more of a whirl than ever.

'Well, you know what happens when cattle stray and a car comes behind them. They just run in front of it, and it's driving them along all the time. That's what must have happened, but the trouble was I didn't know which way he'd gone.'

She didn't need to describe her feelings. I could imagine them.

'I ran up the hill, yelling his name. It seemed quite hopeless, but I didn't stop to think. Then it was like a miracle. He suddenly appeared over the brow of the hill. He came running down towards me with a big van behind him.'

'But how did he come to turn back?' I asked.

'It was the mobile butcher's van, and the butcher stopped to explain what had happened. Apparently the other car had sent Tim right up the hill, all the way to the crossroads, and the butcher's van was just turning into our road when they got there. When he saw Tim he stopped and said to the other driver, "He belongs at the bottom. I'll take him back." It was so good of him. He drove slowly all the way down the hill, sending Tim on in front of him.'

'And how long did all this take?' I asked.

'Less than ten minutes. Poor old Tim, he must have run up that hill. He certainly beat Darkie at it!'

Darkie, I pointed out, drew a cart behind her, and was never foolish enough to try and run races with cars. I added that I hoped Tim was none the worse.

'Just tired. He wanted to get on the straw and flop. He must have gone after that bramble along the hedge, and I don't believe he thought it was worth it.'

Poor Tim! Comforting billy goats is not in my line, and he would not have lacked a cuddle from his mistress, but I wished I had been there on his safe return home. And most certainly to have cuddled Susy on her return from the vet.

So one way and another, when I left the telephone kiosk I was feeling quite homesick. How real they all seemed, my little family, and yet how far away! As far away as regards seeing them as if many miles separated us. And I was no longer a carefree traveller with no ties, unconscious of time, but a weary one upon whom time weighed heavily.

I thought of the small house in its large garden, so very dear because it was *home*. For over fifty autumns pounded like a ship at sea by fierce gales straight off the Atlantic, it had yet stood out every storm, and when we bought it a few years ago it looked as good as when it had been built. Those apparently frail timbers had a stout endurance. How like the human frame in diverse circumstances! That little house could well see another fifty autumns, never mind fifteen.

I found myself thinking of all the other houses I had lived in over the past seventy-odd years. There were too many to count on the fingers of two hands, for like the nomad I do not seem to have put down roots anywhere. As a child we moved from one rented house to another, owing to my father's work, and once I went into service I continued to move from place to place. Twice again on marriage, and later five times more.

There was the little house with the stream at the bottom of the garden, the tall house with the flight of steps and a basement, the house by the railway line, and the big houses that were my week's work to clean. A dark downstairs flat like an underground cavern so often brightened by merry-making on wartime reunions. An upstairs flat with a balcony and window-boxes overflowing with greenery and flowers.

Then a semi-detached house down a lane that always seemed to be muddy, where the scent of innumerable wild roses was sweet in June and birds sang all day long. A terrace house in a town, cottages in the country . . . I could fill an estate agent's window with details. The only house I could not remember was where I was born. A room over a baker's shop in Shoreditch, which we left when I was still a baby, so I was fortunate in being bred a country child.

I was sitting now on high downs overlooking the sea. It was our supper-time, Darkie's and mine. Not far away was the farmhouse that would accommodate us that night, so I was free to take my ease in the last of the evening sun before descending to bed. To take my ease, to fill my eyes and mind with the beauty of earth, sky and sea, to think and dream, and to linger till the approaching dusk reminded me again of time.

Like Dreaming John of Grafton who sat in the sunset amid a shining company of Nature spirits, I too seemed no longer alone. Down the years they came flocking back, the people of my memories, crowding upon me out of the houses of the past.

No fantasy this! Practical and realistic they came.

'Here's me head, me behind's coming!' sang out my father of the stable boy who helped him with the horses that pulled the van on his wholesale oil round. (Only he didn't use so polite a word as behind.) Jack, notoriously slow, creeping about his work around the stables, often came in for that remark. My robust father with the curling moustaches had not lost any of the nimbleness of his young days when he had been a jockey, despite the fact that he had put on considerable weight since then. Probably owing to my mother's cooking!

Out of the kitchen door came the entrancing smells . . . enormous beef stews topped with dumplings in the old iron pot; fat pork sausages plump with rich meat, making a merry sizzle; meat puddings with the gravy oozing brown under the crust; pancakes with lashings of sugar and lemon; spotted-dog suety puddings crammed with currants; delicious pie dish rice puddings slow-baked in the oven alongside the coal fire . . . the meals my mother made! She never worried about calories or vitamins or weight watching, only about filling us up, especially during the cold winters. And

117

she herself remained as willowy as ever under her long, swishing black skirts, graceful as a ballroom dancer as she went about her work with broom and pail and duster.

She was proud that my father had once been a jockey, and would say to me, 'In his young days your father would send his mother home a hundred pounds at a time.' A hundred pounds all at once! What a fortune it had seemed – a fortune indeed in the 1880s compared with today. One hundred golden sovereigns to count and jingle and feel heavy in one's purse. And so romantic because the money had come from across the Channel, all the way from France, from the French stables where my father had spent several years.

And then suddenly there was the Frenchman at the back door of our English house with the strings of onions across his shoulder, jabbering and gesticulating to my mother, and

my father shouting from inside the house, 'Don't you buy them, Toots! I'll beat the beggar down to a fair price. I know his lingo!'

Again I was listening admiringly to the unintelligible discourse, thinking how clever my father was, watching the wheedling onion seller, seeing him shrug, seeing onions and money change hands – at my father's price.

'Daisy, Daisy!' called a child's voice across the years. 'Daisy, your father's had an accident and been taken to the hospital, and your mother's gone to see him.'

Children were always teasing one another so the first cold fear was gone in an instant as I called back defensively, 'Don't be silly! Of course he hasn't.'

'He has, he has!' she insisted, and frightened again I ran home – to an empty house, there to await my mother's return.

The accident had happened on a steep flight of stone steps at the back of a shop. My father was going down them backwards, a five-gallon can of oil in each hand, when he lost his footing, falling down that flight and then somersaulting over a rail down another flight on to the road below. He was still conscious when a policeman arrived on the scene, and managed to express urgent concern for the safety of his money bag.

It was the weekend. When my mother came home she said, 'You can go to the hospital on Sunday.'

We all went on Sunday, and I remember how upset I felt when I saw my father in bed with his head bandaged. Yet no one realised at that time the seriousness of his injuries. During the following year he was to have persistent headaches, and I have vivid memories of watching him fling himself down on the steps outside our house and pressing his head against the cold stone in an effort to obtain some relief.

One day we went to London to see my aunt. I was enchanted with the scene from the top of a bus – a bus with no roof, and a waterproof covering attached to the seat to wrap over our legs if it rained. It was dusk, and the lights everywhere fascinated me. Then suddenly I saw it – my name, brightly lit up in big letters. The combination of my own name and what it said underneath seemed pure magic. A magic answer, indeed, for my poor father.

'Look, dad, look! You needn't have headaches any more!'

He turned to look, and read 'DAISY POWDERS FOR HEADACHES'. I wondered how he could be so sure when he said wryly, 'They won't do my head any good.'

In June that year he must have had some premonition of what would happen in August, for he realised a life-long ambition. Ever since he had been a jockey in France he had wanted to see an English Derby run, and he had never achieved that ambition. That year he took a day off from

119

work and went. When he came back I had never seen him look happier.

Came August, and his sudden collapse into pneumonia. He was to go into hospital, and the Salvation Army band were playing down the street. 'Shall I ask them to stop, Dad?' I suggested.

He shook his head, 'No, let them play.'

He wanted to get up to look after his horses, and my mother had to assure him that she would see to it that Jack gave them proper attention. When the ambulance came he got out of bed, put a blanket round him, and walked downstairs. He refused to be carried out of the house. At the gate he turned, casting back one long, searching look. This memory has remained with me all my life. Soon afterwards he lost consciousness, only regaining it for a few moments just before he died. He repeated the Lord's prayer line by line after the clergyman at his bedside, and as soon as it was said lapsed into unconsciousness again.

I was at home waiting for my grandmother to arrive. And there we were, she and I, walking together down the street to go to the hospital, only to meet my mother and little brother walking back towards us. My father had died at the age of forty-one.

Yes, grief is a strong emotion, I reflected. It tears and obliterates and paralyses. At the time it fills the world, and we are unable to look beyond that time. Strength comes, comfort sometimes, rarely understanding. Yet if we sought to understand and interpret life itself at such times our grief would be less devastating. Life is a moving creation, and we too must move on in our minds, passing willingly from one phase to another. Not looking back regretfully to our memories but taking our memories with us into each new phase, taking our loved ones too by our very thoughts of them. Sometimes on a journey we do not always walk side by side; one or two go ahead, someone turns aside to explore; the children run, playing. And life too is a journey.

I was back in the present. The sun had made a golden pathway across the sea. On the sunset side of it, I would perhaps have liked to follow it into the land of the sunrise. Yet why! The end of a day is often more satisfying than the beginning, and there is comfort to be had in the dark place of the night when you make peace within yourself. Peace from the commotion of the day, even from the commotion of a thought-laden mind.

I looked towards Darkie, and smiled. She and I had good beds awaiting us after our day's excursion and we would both sleep the sweeter for all our outdoor activity. Yet for me the night would undoubtedly mean another excursion, for after the mental journey I had made back into the past I would certainly walk again with those remembered ones in my dreams. The only doubt seemed to be how much of this I would recall when I woke in the morning.

NEXT morning I was on the road with the past so far behind me that it had no place in my mind. Again I was homesick! I wanted to be back in our little house with my present-day family, to walk in the garden under the trees, to thrill again to that circle of skyline that seems to enclose us so safely.

I pictured it all. The two white goats on the green grass with brown King Billy, his long beard golden in the sun. Bettybunny popping through the pig-wire fence to her favourite clover patch. Susy at her latest occupation, tumbling the logs about as she sniffed and scratched, and cats emerging here and there from cool places.

In my ears was the voice of the wood pigeon in the tall fir trees, and the cheeky shouting of the chaffinches from the willow tree; even the slight crackling like old parchment as a little wind stirred the ornamental grass.

There in my remembering was the red post office van at the gate . . . the radio to switch on for the one o'clock news. And there on the veranda stood my afternoon chair. All the outdoor sounds, from the stirring of the grasses to the occasional helicopter, which always sends the goats to flatten themselves against the fence. And drifting from the kitchen Freda's conversation with the cats. 'Mind then, little Ball, sweet-pie Ball . . . and you, Tom. Now *mind*, Tom Darling Purr, I've got things to do . . . Oh, Twinkle, what is it now? Drink of milk? Just a minute then . . . Drinky, drinky, little Twinkie . . .'

'Oh Darkie!' I said suddenly. 'I want to go home!'

She plodded on as if she had not heard, and in the very moment of thinking that I might just as well cut short my journey and return that very day I remembered that at home there were five cats instead of six. I had set out with a purpose. If I had to return without news of Matilda it would not be because I had not completed the journey. Every planned call should be made.

In fact I made more calls. I stopped at cottages as well as farms; I asked people I met. But who could be expected to notice one small black and white cat when there were so many cats everywhere?

A woman said, 'I've been feeding a stray cat for days, but I don't know if it's a he or a she. Come and have a look.'

Now I had a wonderful opportunity – something I had always wanted to do! 'Can I give you a lift?' I asked.

She was delighted. 'I've never had a lift in a donkey cart before!'

On the way to her cottage she told me that she was often given a lift. Generally in a car, but she had also ridden on the back of a boy's fast motor cycle, in the cab of a lorry, on a trailer behind a tractor – but never in a donkey cart. And on arrival at the green gate of her white-washed cottage she gave it as her opinion that this was the most satisfying ride she had ever had.

There was no cat to be seen as we went up the path.

'It'll be here somewhere,' she said. 'It never goes far away. Round the back, I expect. Puss, puss, puss!'

A series of miaows answered her.

'Oh no!' I said at once. 'That isn't Matilda.'

She looked at me in surprise. 'How ever can you tell without looking at it?'

'The voice,' I said. 'It isn't Matilda's voice.'

'Well now!' she said. 'And I thought all cats sounded the same when they miaowed.'

'We've got six,' I told her, laughing, 'and whichever one I heard outside the door I'd know at once who it was.'

'Well, I never!' she said.

Yet it is easy enough, as easy as knowing the difference in their temperaments. Matilda, the eldest, has a distinct but modulated miaow, as near to that spelling as anyone might wish. Fairy, the youngest, produces an ear-splitting banshee wail – perhaps befitting a cat born wild – with which she has haunted many a still summer afternoon when, more active than her sleeping elders, she has found herself walking alone in the lane. For Fairy likes company.

Teenie gives a little quiet cry, Tom Purry a high-pitched

one. Twinkle manages a rather endearing soft murmur that is almost a chuckle. And Fluffball's contribution is just a small open mouth from which only the faintest sound has ever been known to issue, and that rarely.

The black and white cat emerged from behind a water butt, greeting my companion affectionately by rubbing against her legs. As she bent to stroke it I smiled, glad that at least one stray cat had found a friend. 'You'll be adopting that one,' I said.

I went on my way marvelling at the diversity of black and white cats. The number I had seen! And never in exact detail did they match Matilda's markings. So I let my thoughts relax for a little while as I contemplated the individuality of things. How pleasant it is to take time off in this way from problems, from the devouring tensions and crises in the world that would swallow our peace, or what little peace most people have in modern society.

Even the blades of grass, I reflected, looking at the green bank, were individual. At a casual glance along the length of the bank they might appear to be identical, all close together in a great mass of grass like people in a crowd. Yet each had its own portion of root, and each grew in its own way. I had only to stop and investigate and I would find this was so. They would be different heights, even if only by fractions, different widths too, and bearing signs of their life's tale – the nibbled, the weather-browned edged, the straight and the bowed. Yet in their individuality they grew so close they were as one plant.

How great a loss it is when we forget the magic of the earth. When there is no longer any wonder left in us. Perhaps we know too much – or is it too little? – when we fail to be moved by the miracle of creation.

I played a child's game on my slow journey – a version, perhaps, of the old 'I-Spy'. I looked for individual things in the great whole of earth and sky and then for identification on the individual. A wisp of white cloud that spread and ruffled itself like a little pair of wings until I could almost see the feathers; a blackberry flower tinged delicately mauve and so large it stood out from the rest and made me wonder how big the berry would be. Two striped caterpillars on a nettle, one surely fat enough to burst its skin while the other had a good deal more eating to do. Interesting crannies between the grey and ivied stone that revealed itself here and there on the bank, and as surely as I sat in the cart in one cranny a bold, bright eye. Or was it perhaps a sparkle in the stone? I didn't stop to investigate so I never knew, though I enjoyed the thought of a small inhabitant in the cranny.

So many little individual things . . . they reminded me of a girl I once knew. Quite a young girl, just married. Slim, red-haired, eyes full of dreams. So little to do in her brand new house on the edge of a common that she spent half her day walking a scrap of a dog over the grass, among the gorse, up and down the hillocks, and through the silver birch spinneys where in autumn scarlet toadstools grew. In summer the common was covered in flowers of many kinds, and each time I met her she had a tiny posy.

'I pick the smallest flowers,' I remembered her saying. 'You see, I only want a tiny bunch.' And in her hand would be harebells, ladies' slippers, daisies, scarlet pimpernels. She was well aware of things like fairy circles on the grass and mused with me one April evening between sun and shower about the end of the rainbow. One day she went to work in a tall house in the town. She looked sad in the streets of the town, but I never knew her story, except that she walked no more across the common.

Here was another miracle . . . an old woman's memory that could conjure a small forgotten incident out of a past packed with incidents, big and small, and present it life-size in all its original enchantment. Girl, dog, green and lovely common, flowers, and atmosphere all complete, and with it that faint sense of wistfulness and mystery stealing back to me over the years.

She would be old now – yet how could so young and romantic a girl ever be old? Surely her spirit walked that common still. In her heart she must have been there many times, gathering her small posies again. So how can we mourn lost youth when in the wisdom of age we know that we ourselves, within our wrinkled bodies, are ageless? No one can deny us our knowledge – we know indisputably how we *feel*!

The sun was hot; Darkie had stopped. I climbed out of the cart and drew her in where a field gateway was set back between the hedges and tied her securely. It was as good a place as any to stop for lunch, and we would not be long. Or so I thought! While Darkie stood in reverie after hers I dropped asleep after mine, and woke with no idea how long we had been there. I had slipped into a comfortable hollow by the gatepost, and half opening my eyes looked at tall grasses towering, it seemed, like a little forest, above my head. Tall flowering grasses, each one different.

Some had little knobs, others had plumes. Others again had tassels, and there were some that looked as if they had clusters of very tiny beads. The colour tones were more distinct than I had ever noticed before. Quiet, subdued grass colours; reddish purples, greys and fawns and half-shades, the dark and the light and the unexpected richness, a whole gentle community of grasses swaying together in air moving so lightly that I, beneath them, could not feel it.

Too drowsy to move from so pleasant a place, I watched them, and they seemed to me as alive as a community of people within their world of the field's edge, communicating with each other as they danced their summer dance. It was so soothing to lie there, and I prolonged it until disturbed from my reverie by a white monster nosing past the donkey cart.

There was plenty of room for the car to pass as we had drawn in, yet it did not pass. It remained level with the cart, and sitting up I craned to see why. Someone in the car was craning too, his attention riveted upon Darkie, who turned her face to scrutinise him in turn. Well . . . nothing unusual about *that*. Everybody looked at the donkey, and he, apparently, was so absorbed in her that he did not notice me sitting against the gatepost.

A honk from behind finally got him moving, and when the two cars had gone I bestirred myself to continue the journey. We had not gone far before we came to a lay-by and there, drawn in, was the white car. The driver was reading a newspaper, which he at once laid down as we drew level. I glanced down to acknowledge him, but again he was not looking at me. He had eyes only for the donkey.

For some reason I jerked the reins and murmured to her to get along. And then we were by, and I forgot the incident. But I had not seen the last of the white car, for a few minutes later there it was again, just behind us. I drew in as close as I could to the left and waved my hand. Nothing happened. The white car had stopped too, and was not starting again.

I was slightly irritated. After waiting a moment or two longer I got Darkie moving. It was even more irritating when after we had gone a few yards the car started up and began crawling behind us.

For the first time I found myself wishing that Darkie would gallop! Oh, for uplifted hooves and the cart flying along behind, the astonished car driver changing gear and then a track down which we would vanish, a track quite unsuited to a sleek white car!

The track, at any rate, came. Round a bend we went, and the car lingered behind, presumably to allow us time to get round it, and when we were round it there it was – a cart track sloping up into a wood.

On an impulse I halted Darkie, climbed out of the cart and led her up. We were disappearing among the trees when the white car went along the bottom.

'Well, Darkie,' I said, 'that's that! I suppose it was a foolish thing to do, but I feel triumphant!'

I celebrated by sitting on a log and eating my last piece of chocolate, while Darkie ate her next-to-last carrot. 'My goodness!' I said. 'It's a good thing tomorrow is our last day. We're running out of provisions!'

I was feeling quite light-hearted as I led her down the woodland track, for we would have the lane to ourselves again and tomorrow was the last lap of our journey. And, who knew, at the eleventh hour I might even find Matilda.

As to what happened after that I cannot describe it. I have no idea exactly what *did* happen. One moment I was leading Darkie down the slope and turning into the lane, the next she was sprawling on the ground with the cart on its side behind her.

I was so shocked I could only stand and stare, and then my concern for her got me moving. She was struggling to get up, and having difficulty, strapped as she was between the shafts. I tried to help her, but it seemed I had no strength. The first thing to do seemed to be to get the cart the right way up again, and I couldn't do that either.

It was a frightening sight, Darkie on the ground and the cart toppled over like a toy. I had no idea what to do. The lane was empty, and could remain so indefinitely. I could not go for help and leave her there.

She was as calm as ever, persevering in her endeavour to get to her feet. She it was who soothed me rather than I her. No need for me to say, 'It's all right, Darkie, never mind', though I *did* say it, for she behaved as if getting up from a sitting position in the middle of the road, hampered by a topsy-turvy cart, was an everyday occurrence. My chief anxiety was that she had hurt herself, though it did not appear so.

The answer to the problem came – unexpected and ironic. We were to be rescued from our predicament by he who had all unwittingly caused it – the driver of the white car!

Softly it slid towards us. Slowly it stopped. Unhurriedly the door opened and the driver stepped out, smiling and unperturbed.

By now Darkie had struggled to her feet, but the cart remained on its side.

'So glad to meet up with you again,' said the driver of the car. 'I couldn't think where you'd gone. Not having trouble, are you?'

'If you could just help me – ' I began, pushing at the cart.

'Of course.' He hastened to do so, and after a moment we had the cart firmly upright on its two wheels again. For the first time I realised that half its contents were scattered on the ground. Between us we salvaged them. The only casualty was the biscuit tin, which had been squashed flat.

He held it in his hands, looking at it in a puzzled way. Until then I don't think he had quite realised what had happened, any more than I had taken stock of him as he approached. I saw now that he was middle-aged and well-dressed.

'Two things I never expected to see,' he remarked. 'One, a donkey cart. Two, an accident to a donkey cart.' He looked at me. 'You must have had a shake up.'

I felt more shame-faced than shaken as I explained what had happened. I had taken a fancy to go up into the woods, I said, and on the way down the slope to the road Darkie had stumbled and the cart had tipped over. But I wasn't in it, as I was leading her.

He appeared not to be listening. Again all his attention was given to Darkie, as it had been when he first passed us.

'Do you want to sell that donkey?' he asked.

I was almost indignant. 'Sell her? I haven't long bought her!'

'I could write you a cheque now,' he said. 'Then if you give me your address I could arrange to have her picked up.'

I looked at Darkie and the cart. Both appeared to be none the worse for our mishap. The time had clearly come to start moving. With an alacrity that surprised even me I climbed into the cart and took the reins.

'If you want a donkey,' I said, 'I hope you will soon find one for sale. This one isn't.' I gave the reins a little jerk. 'On you go, Darkie!'

Borne away from him by four hooves and two wheels, I fixed my gaze to the tips of Darkie's ears and tried to regain a little dignity. But the severity of our departure seemed slightly unjust, so I called back as sincerely as I could, 'Thank you for helping us!'

Us . . . Yes, we were a pair, Darkie and I. Partners in our outdoor life. I was as much dependent upon her as she was

9

upon me. It would take more than a cheque book to separate us! Nothing within my control would ever do so. And I liked to think that her desire would be the same as my control. For were we not true companions, Darkie and I? We understood each other; we belonged.

'Perhaps, Darkie,' I said, 'it's just as well we're going home tomorrow!'

TOMORROW came – in the guise, of course, of 'today' – and what a day! I woke in my farmhouse bedroom to windows patterned with raindrops and a wind curling the flying tendrils of clematis that had escaped their trellis.

Why should the sight of raindrops on the window cause the heart to sink? As long as I could remember it had been so. As a child, waking, the doleful cry, 'Oh, a wet day!' and later, gazing out at a garden which looked lace-curtained from the house, 'Rain, rain go away, come again another day!'

And would we chanting children have been any more pleased to see the rain on that other day?

As with so many things our feelings were based on our own comfort, our personal desires. It did not concern us that the roots of the trees were soaking up the downpour, the grass growing greener. Wryly I told myself these things as I watched the rain that morning before stirring out of bed. I made a new commandment – 'Let not thy heart sink with the rain, but rather lift up thy spirits.'

'Sister Rain,' said St Francis. One welcomes a sister. Outside all was refreshment because the rain had come; inside, comfortably dry in bed, I could admire my diamond patterned window pane.

'Will you stay awhile?' suggested the kindly farmer's wife after breakfast.

Would I stay awhile? The prospect was tempting. But if I did my plans for the day would come to nothing, and inattentive as I am to time the fever to go home was upon me. I must reach there by dusk.

'It isn't really *much*,' I said, going to the window to convince myself. 'I think we'll be on our way.'

And thanking her for her hospitality I went out into the

131

rainswept morning to break the news to Darkie.

No, it wasn't much as we set off. I think Darkie agreed with me, for she stepped out well, and I was glad we had started. The rain now was all in the wind, wet streamers of it flying lightly by, almost passing over our heads, it seemed, I well wrapped and hooded and she under her waterproof with only her ears and nose exposed to the elements.

Who would have guessed we had so longed-for a destination as we loitered along? So familiar had I become with the sight of a stretch of road ahead that even I felt as if this journey had no end, as if we would for ever make our way along these winding lanes, as if, indeed, we had become part of our surroundings. Not a foot of lane did we traverse without awareness, except for the dreaming times. Not for us the fleeting flash of hedge flying past, the barest glimpse of colour in it, a gateway with an entrancing view over which we could not look our fill. We saw everything there was to see, yet even we at donkey pace missed much. There is always more to see than ever hedge or grass or landscape reveals to the casual passer-by.

We had two more calls to make that day – the last enquiries in my attempt to find Matilda. How easy on a bright day to have anticipated success, a happy homecoming. As it was my spirits had failed to conquer the weather, and there was I, hunched in mackintosh, brooding

dismally over the situation even while I took care not to miss anything the journey might have to offer.

But I do dislike being cut off from the sky. The low clouds made a grey roof over my head, shutting out the great open expanse of the heavens, and my thoughts were earthbound. The two calls I had to make would both prove fruitless, as all the others had been, and as far as finding Matilda was concerned I might just as well not have set out on this journey at all, I forgot all its pleasures and interest and little adventures, even forgot to direct my erring thoughts, and went so far as to think it had been a foolish venture totally unsuited to one of my age, that I had only wearied myself for nothing and that it would have been better to have returned home yesterday before the rain.

Home . . . and where was the joyous homecoming? Weary and dispirited, I could not even anticipate *that*. I found that I was taking it for granted, that the meaning had gone out of everything. And then my thoughts, as thoughts do, began to enlarge and embroider, and I was thinking of life's journey and the end of it. Did we come to the end of it like this, ceasing to care for very weariness, conscious only of failure when we looked back down the long road of the years?

I then wondered who can assess failure if, in being conscious of it, we see only a corner of the picture we think we are looking at. On this journey of mine I had set out to find a cat. The chances were, had been from the beginning, that I would not find her. But I had searched faithfully and I would complete the journey. It had also rewarded me with many experiences I would not otherwise have had, and in one instance at least – when I had met the children and later gone with them to see little Lindy – it had brought happiness to others.

There had been one mistake which might have been serious when I had gone up the track into the woods, and we had had the mishap on the downward bit. If Darkie had been hurt or the cart damaged I would have blamed myself. Yet I had not foreseen the consequences of that action of leaving the road. It had taught me to take more care in future. In order to realise this I had first had to make my mistake. So looking back on all the apparent failures and mistakes on the longer journey of life itself I realised they had been made because at the time of making them I was not, at that stage, capable of doing anything else, and each had given me some experience I would not otherwise have had. Through some of those experiences I had grown inwardly in a way that I could now see plainly, and I felt that others which appeared on looking back empty of any significance would reveal much more to me as I went on living.

That was it then! *As I went on living.* I had been thinking only of the end of the journey, the homecoming. But once I had arrived at the end of this donkey journey it did not all stop at the reunion, for another day would dawn. I would walk the garden paths, harness Darkie for more travels, see, hear and do many things. It seemed then that ends always lead to beginnings. Resting places, yes – but never dead ends. No need to be dispirited at all, and the weariness was but a temporary thing.

My Sunday school self of many years ago started to sing.

> Here we suffer grief and pain,
> Here we meet to part again.
> In Heaven we part no more.
> Oh, won't it be joyful,
> Joyful, joyful, joyful,
> Oh, won't it be joyful
> When we meet to part no more.

And there was my uncle's voice again, changing the words just like he used to do.

> Here we suffer grief and pain,
> Over the road it's just the same,
> Next door they suffer more.
> Oh, won't it be joyful ...

His well remembered, boisterous baritone filled my mind, and I lifted my head and found myself saying to Darkie, 'Come on, Darkie – let's smile!' And there it was – the combination of the humorous touch transmuting too much solemnity, and the sudden idea of a *donkey smiling* making me actually burst out laughing.

I completed that morning's drive in good spirits, and by lunch time the rain had gone. Our waterproofs removed, Darkie and I rested contentedly in the sunshine.

W E made our two calls, and there was now no more hope of finding Matilda on that journey. Confronted by this cold fact, I was isolated for a moment in the sense of finality which such situations create. One stands, as it were, on the brink of the known world, and everything but the one fact that has presented itself to the mind falls away.

Rare indeed to experience this. For it is not only modern lives that are so crammed with detail and activity, but the overcrowded minds of the people living them. And so often it is grief or shock or some sadness that brings us to the edge of thought and halts us there. Happiness radiates and is fulfilling; it is inclusive, not isolating, bringing all the world to our feet, but these other moments, brief and bare, separate us and bring a clarity that seems strange to a mind so used to being filled and jostled by unceasing thoughts. Like stepping out of a crowded room on to a hilltop.

A moment, perhaps, not to abhor but to hold? From the depth of such a moment to what height might we not reach if we but find the way? But usually we gravitate to the crowded earth, the mind swings back to its teeming multitudes of waiting thoughts.

Back behind my plodding donkey I was only half wistfully aware of a moment that might have expanded had I not plunged immediately into my thought stream. But there it was, the same old thinking process going over it all again. The end of the journey, said my thoughts, but not the desired result . . . Where was she . . . what had happened . . . would she ever come back . . . ?

I looked down at my imperturbable donkey steadfastly pursuing her way, as yet unaware that she was going home. She immediately relaxed me, as she always does.

'Darkie,' I said, 'we're going home!'

135

And then, of course, she stopped!

'Home!' I repeated firmly, and flicked the reins. Did I detect an added briskness to her step, a sudden buoyancy, as if those gentle hooves had springs hidden within? Very likely it was all within my own heart, for the word 'home' now rekindled my desire for it. I had been away long enough.

What a long journey it seemed now, looking back. Centuries might have passed instead of one little week. A week crowded with incidents and filled with memories. And that night I would sleep in my own familiar bed, and it would feel strange to me – in fact all the dear familiarity of home would come new to me after my journey out into the world. I was returning with a broader vision, a deepening consciousness of the things that matter.

All being well we should arrive long before dusk. The closing of the day would find me safely within doors, sitting again in the lamp-light; weary no doubt but content. And then I fell to musing, and I thought how even one day alone, each individual day in fact, embodies in it the pattern of our complete life-time, from birth to death – and beyond. At daybreak we wake. Our consciousness is born again into the world. Morning brings many activities. By afternoon much is in order, we are well established in the day and can look back on what we have achieved or left undone. But there is still more to do. Evening brings relaxation – now we are getting old and like to put our feet up. Then night and sleep; and as we close our eyes and drift into it we have 'died' in our consciousness to the world we know as surely as if the link had been finally severed. We are not afraid to sleep, for we know we shall wake again. And what timeless regions lie beyond sleep? They may well await our exploration, even as this world does – yet have we not been there before, and will they not have all the familiarity of home?

We were returning by way of the woods – not along the lane that runs through them but a track above, which I call the skyline path. Here I seem to be on the very top of the world, looking down upon the woods and feeling very close to the sky. On one side the wooded valley, its trees and fields climbing a hillside to another skyline, the deep lane sunk between hedges of hazel and honeysuckle, elderberry, ash, beech and oak. Opening out on the other side as we make our way along are hundreds of fields stretching to the coastline, and right around is the embrace of the sky, making its complete circle unbroken at any point and giving that lovely illusion of reaching down to meet the earth.

Here was the kestrel's haunt, and the bird that would have appeared as a speck from the lane below now looked not far above my head as he hovered in the still air. Near enough to have that fleeting, exciting glimpse of a face.

Then we came to my favourite place. Here we look down upon our own timbered bungalow, almost a little toy house set down there among the fields. I thrilled to see it again, and from my vantage point watched for signs of activity.

There were the two white goats grazing in the middle of the field. The brown billy was not so easy to spot, but presently he emerged from the hedge. A tiny spot of white in the field I took to be Bettybunny, having her evening meal from the clover patch. The cats were probably in the lane, and I would see them on my way up, and I guessed where Susy was – inside the bungalow, being prepared for my homecoming.

'Now guess who's coming – listen! Are you listening?' Here her head would be instantly on one side, one ear pricked. 'You can go and look in a minute – no, in a minute. Not *now*, in a minute. And you're going to say hallo nicely, aren't you? Nicely, mind ...'

Would they glance up and see me there, outlined against the sky? They would be expecting me along the bottom lane, and there were doubtless preparations for my arrival going on. I began to look forward to my supper. It would be everything I liked, of course – I hazarded a guess at scrambled egg and lettuce, lemon jelly and fruit cake.

Now I knew I had lingered too long. It was not yet dusk, but there was that lovely light over the fields that immediately precedes it, a mingling of sunset and moon glow making the last of the vanishing daylight shine. I had promised to be there at the bottom of our own little lane before dusk, all being well. Soon they would be waiting for me.

I just about made it. Susy was the first to greet me, rushing up the hill to meet the donkey cart as soon as she saw it, and Freda was not far behind. The cats were sitting in our lane, one behind the other, but I could not pretend that this was a deputation to welcome me, for it is their habit to sit there like that in the evening.

'Eric's coming to unharness her for you,' said Freda, when we reached the field gate. It was really stable time, but we let Darkie into the field for a few minutes, and then stood to watch her reaction to being home. The goats had already gone in so the field was empty. She behaved as she always did, as if she had been away only for an hour or two. Up to the top of the field and then, when she was unharnessed, over to her favourite patch of earth, where she rolled. Darkie had come home.

The kettle, they told me, was boiling, but I had to go and see the goats and find Bettybunny. I was just in time for her going home game, and when she was safely in I went indoors to supper and to tell them some of my adventures.

So much to tell, I was still talking afterwards when I sat in the kitchen while Freda prepared the cats' supper. They were all there – all, that is, save one.

From tumbling kittens leaping from chair to table, stretching out eager paws to hook a snippet of meat falling from kitchen scissors to plate, they have learned to wait patiently. Six good helpings take a little time to prepare. There may be meat to scrape off bones, raw meat to cut, fish bones to remove, and the whole concoction moistened and mixed with their favourite crushed dog biscuit, to say nothing of attention having to be paid to individual likes and dislikes – those who like their meal cooked and those who prefer it raw!

Tom Purry, sleek and black, with his own especial little air of quiet dignity, sitting upright and still on the rug while tiny white Fairy fussed around with busy tongue washing his face. We laugh at this – it is always the black cats she washes.

Twinkle sat bolt upright on the chair nearest the table, watching the food preparations without once relaxing his green-eyed gaze. A vast improvement in behaviour this. He it was who, as a kitten, often had to be banished from the room till supper was ready, so persistent was he in climbing on the table. Black like Tom, but long-haired, and his tiny white shirt-front reminded me that night that it was a miniature of his mother's.

Teenie, the tortoise-shell, sat on the windowsill, staring out into that fascinating darkness of the garden she had just left, and on the arm of Susy's chair sat Fluffball, a bundle of grey fur, as watchful as anyone although he has only one eye. This pale amber eye was fixed on Freda, and I knew he would not stay on the chair arm much longer. And there he was – flying through the air to land effortlessly and with surprising lightness and grace upon her shoulder, then lying full-length across the back of her neck, looking over one shoulder at the food on the table.

How secure I felt in the lamp-lit kitchen. Yet that persistent inner thinking reminded me again that this was not really security, that security comes only from within one's own being. All this in the kitchen could change, even as there were now five cats instead of six. Life was not a static picture of cats in a kitchen and a tired old woman resting from a donkey drive. Life was a moving thing, and because it moved it changed, and I would go along with it, not reluctantly, not in the resignation of despair, but with adventuring spirit. For age has little to do with it; to live is always to adventure onward.

So soon now would come the magic words. They each made a stir of expectancy as the preceding words came. 'There's good ones! Won't be long now. Soon be ready!'

I believe the reason cats are not credited with being as intelligent as dogs is not a true lack of intelligence, but simply that ordinarily they do not listen. They do not listen because they do not want to listen. They are usually engrossed in what they are doing or dreaming about, or where they are going or what they are going to do next. Dogs are more concerned with what their owners are doing or are going to do. But as far as listening is concerned Susy as a puppy was just like a cat – she would not listen. She was at that time far too busy exploring the wonderful world awaiting her discovery.

'She doesn't even *listen*!' we'd cry, after fruitless efforts to instruct her. She must have been all of two years old before she paid any real attention, and what we found most amusing then was that one of the words she very quickly learned was 'Listen!' This can always be relied upon to rivet her attention – eyes expectant, head on one side, one ear raised.

The cats at supper time not only watch, but *listen*. They know every encouraging word that Freda says, every tone of voice that indicates how much nearer supper is coming. And the final sentence is electric and the instant result has to be seen to be believed.

'Now is everybody ready?'

Before she has picked up a plate every cat in the kitchen has moved – leaping from chair or windowsill or shoulder, walking, running, murmuring. There they all are gathered at her feet, each face uplifted, awaiting the descent of the plates.

With the plates come the names, and as only two plates can be lowered at a time each cat waits for its own plate.

'Teenie and Twinkle, Tom Purry and Fluffball, Matilda and Fairy!'

It began in that order when Teenie and Twinkle were the youngest kittens and therefore the most impatient. Matilda as the eldest came last, and as little Fairy was the final arrival she got added on at the end of the list.

But that night it would again be, 'Teenie and Twinkle, Tom Purry and Fluffball – and Fairy.' Matilda's plate remained in the cupboard.

There they were, expectantly waiting, poised in readiness for the next words. And then it happened.

Was it a miaow outside the door? Were we dreaming? But even as Freda looked at me and I at her every cat in the room looked at the door. And then it came again. An unmistakable miaow – Matilda's miaow. This time it was followed by an urgent scratching.

Freda rushed to the door and flung it open, and there was Matilda herself, giving a little cry of greeting and almost falling into the room. As Freda cried, 'Matilda! It's Matilda!' Susy came bounding out of the next room, bouncing and slithering and wagging and sniffing. Supper forgotten, all five cats crowded round, leaving Susy to sniff the tail end while they extended delicate, quivering noses to other parts of Matilda's fur.

She had eyes for none of them. She was looking up, and miaowing again.

'Oh, Tilda!' said Freda and I simultaneously, each expressing our deep thankfulness, and Freda picked her up for a hug before handing her to me and preparing that sixth plate of supper.

I took her, felt the reality of her, and rejoiced. How unexpectedly things happen. My seeking her had been in vain, but she had come. And what a moment to choose! Timed for supper on the very day of my return. Could any journey have had a happier end?

To say that Matilda was hungry is an understatement. She was starving. Helping after helping disappeared and still she looked for more. She followed it all up with milk in almost equal quantity, and then went to the water dish and drank.

Who could say where she had been, what she had been doing, when she had last eaten? It was sufficient that she was there, safe and apparently quite well and uninjured.

I had her in my arms, content and purring, when, much later, I went to say good night to Darkie. Over the top of the stable door the noses of the two animals met. The cat was not in the habit of kissing the donkey, but she was too blissfully tired and comfortable to take alarm at that other larger nose coming towards her own with so soft a touch.

Star-shine and the quaver of a distant owl. The donkey's large and beautiful eyes seeming to shine like the stars, the cat warm and heavy in my arms. Peace around me and within.

Yet how deep and how real was this peace? As skin-deep as the darkness, which would be gone in the morning? Did the earth and sky alone communicate it to me, or would I have felt it if Matilda had not returned? Even as I asked these questions I knew it to be real and abiding, a lasting treasure, a rock amid the waters of life.

I looked back on the long journey I had made – not the one with Darkie – and marvelled that I had arrived intact at this moment of peace. Little and alone in a vast universe, for does not each one of us, like a tree, do our growing in life alone? Then I touched Darkie's broad brow and remembered the words as if she had spoken to me from out of her long-ago past . . . 'And yet I am not alone . . . '

No, you cannot be alone when you realise you are part of a whole, strengthened, comforted and enriched by the life spirit within your own being, knowing that same life spirit is everywhere, at every step of your journey. From what would we not be saved, here and now, and how fully and abundantly live in this very world we inhabit at this moment if we continuously opened our consciousness to our divine source?

Tomorrow, I promised myself, I would sit in the sun and think about it, Matilda on my lap, Darkie back in her field with the goats. The sweet serenity of a summer day in a garden all around me. Surely it was worth going on a long journey just for the joy of returning home.

And the day after tomorrow? Darkie and I would be on the road again, back to an old, familiar route, yet explorers still.

FRED ARCHER

UNDER THE PARISH LANTERN

'It glows with the magical warmth of the age it re-creates'
Sir Bernard Miles

'Memories of rustic Worcestershire half a century ago, packed with the stuff and speech of village life and the tackle and tools of the farmer's round, illustrated with flesh and blood photographs of dogs and badgers, sprout-pickers and harvesters, that go with the text like pickled onions with cheese'
The Observer

'An almost magical evocation of country life ... in the lost England of the first World War and shortly after'
The Sunday Times

CORONET BOOKS

RECENT NON-FICTION FROM CORONET

FRED ARCHER
- ☐ 17864 7   Under the Parish Lantern   40p
- ☐ 17865 5   The Secrets of Bredon Hill   40p
- ☐ 17863 9   The Distant Scene   40p

TOM MACDONALD
- ☐ 21321 3   The White Lanes of Summer   65p

VERNE MORGAN
- ☐ 19995 4   Yesterday's Sunshine   70p

JEAN RENNIE
- ☐ 21837 1   Every Other Sunday   95p

ERNEST DUDLEY
- ☐ 19877 X   For Love of a Wild Thing   85p

All these books are available at your local bookshop or newsagent, or can be ordered direct from the publisher. Just tick the titles you want and fill in the form below.

Prices and availability subject to change without notice.

CORONET BOOKS, P.O. Box 11, Falmouth, Cornwall.

Please send cheque or postal order, and allow the following for postage and packing:

U.K. – One book 22p plus 10p per copy for each additional book ordered, up to a maximum of 82p.

B.F.P.O. and EIRE – 22p for the first book plus 10p per copy for the next 6 books, thereafter 4p per book.

OTHER OVERSEAS CUSTOMERS – 30p for the first book and 10p per copy for each additional book.

Name ....

Address ....

....